# How'd You do That?

## Volume 1

Poser® Character Creation for Beginners
(Now Updated for Poser8 Users)

By DAD

Copyright 2008-09 DAD

ISBN 1434841197
EAN 13978143481193

# Introduction

Hello, I'm DAD. Some of you out there in Poserdom may know me or at least know of me and you probably have a few of my characters somewhere in your runtime. I've been using Poser since version 2.0 and have been providing 3$^{rd}$ party content since that version too. I am probably one of the first, if not the first, person to provide a fully rigged 3$^{rd}$ party character for use in Poser3. How many of you remember a character called AntiPasto?

My first attempts at making Poser content were pretty pathetic. I was using a software package called Arena3D. Never heard of it? Not surprising. The only file format it exported to that Poser3 could read was DXF. It didn't work very well, but it taught me a lot about how not to do things. And because I made all those mistakes all those years ago, I figured it was about time I taught a few people the easy way to make Poser content. Not only will this book teach you how to do it the easy way, but it will teach you how to do it for FREE.

So, get yourself a cup of coffee, sit back, and jump to the last page of the book to find out where you can get all the cool programs I use to create Poser characters on the Internet for free. Download them and the free content I'm providing at Content Paradise and we'll start building a Poser character together.

Please note, this process has been tested and shown to work in Poser 4Pro thru Poser6 on the PC. Although not tested in Poser7, or 7Pro, or on the Mac, the process should also work as long as they have legacy use of PHI files still active. Mac users will have to use a text editor to create their PHI files.

# Chapter 1: Basic Concepts

As we work our way through the book we will be dealing with several different programs that are needed to prep a model for use in Poser, create a UV map for the model once it is in Poser, and then paint the textures using the UV map so that the character has more than just a plain white skin. The programs we will be using in addition to Poser are as follows:

UVMapper Classic – Used for dividing up the OBJ mesh and for creating the UV Map for painting textures. (Note: When using UVMapper always maximize your screen to give yourself the most work space. Images in the book are cropped for publishing purposes.)

PHI-Builder – Used for creating the import file to get the OBJ into Poser and establishing initial joint parameters.

Artweaver – A very nice paint program similar to Photoshop.

And the nicest thing about the programs listed above is that they are all FREE.

I'm sure some of what I just said went straight over your head but rest assured that I'll explain everything in due course. So let's start with the OBJ mesh.

Poser uses an industry standard Wavefront OBJ mesh for the base structure of the character. Although Poser can import many different types of meshes (Maya, 3DMax, Lightwave, and others), the OBJ mesh is the native format used for all models in the Poser runtime. The OBJ format is a text file that defines locations in 3D space with numerical coordinates. Don't understand that? Don't worry, you don't need to. Just understand that to keep from pulling your hair out, it is best to start with an OBJ formated mesh for creating a Poser character.

Up above I heard some of you scream, "What's a joint parameter?" Ok, let's stand up and take a look at our bodies. Hold your arm out to your side with your palm pointing down. Now bend your arm at the elbow until your hand touches your chest. Now try to bend your arm backwards at the elbow until your hand touches your back. That's a joint parameter. It defines how far a joint in the body can move and how it moves. If you can't physically do it with your body, your character shouldn't be able to do it with theirs.

There are three related settings that help define the joint parameters (JPs) that are called include/exclude angles, spherical blend zones, and limits. The include/exclude angles define the basic area around the joint that is affected by the bending of the joint. The spherical blend zones further define this area by limiting how the area blends together at the joint. The limits are used to keep the joint from spinning out of control and looking like a corkscrew. In many situations the body of a Poser character only requires you to worry about two settings: the include/exclude angles and the limits.

Additionally, when thinking about the body joints and the JPs we also need to think about what is called joint rotation. In Poser joints have three axis' of rotation that they can move on. If you draw three imaginary lines where one is going top to bottom, one is going left to right, and one is going front to back: you have defined the rotations axis'. They are: top to bottom – y Axis, left to right – x Axis, front to back – z Axis. Each of these play an important part in how a JP is initially defined. See Figure 1 - 1.

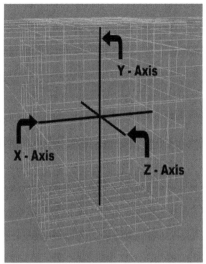

Fig 1-1

The first rotation of ALL joints needs to be what is called the Twist. If you look at your arm when it is held out to your side with the palm down and 'Twist' your arm so the palm faces up, you will note that the arm rotates at the shoulder, elbow, and wrist on a line that runs from left to right through the arm or on the x Axis. If you stand up and 'Twist' your body left and right to look from side to side you will note that the body rotates at the head, neck, chest, and waist on the line that runs from top to bottom or the y Axis. The same is true for your thigh, knee and ankle. The only oddballs that twist on the z Axis are the front part of the foot (and toes), sometimes the thumb joints, the tongue (if it is defined as a moving body part) and on men ... well, we'll skip that part for now.  See Fig 1-1 above for reference.

Since you now have a basic idea of joints and rotations, don't worry we'll go over it again, let's move onto the various programs we'll be using and explain how they are used just a little bit.

**UVMapper Classic** – Written by Steve Cox

UVMapper Classic is probably one of the most important programs you can get for creating Poser content. Not only does it allow you to create UV Maps for painting textures, it allows you to easily divide up a mesh into the basic body groupings, name them, and create material groups for properly texturing your creations without the need of a 3D design program.

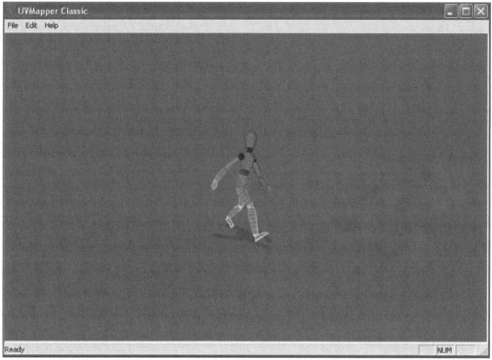

Fig 1-2

The interface, as seen in Figure 1-2, is extremely simple. Don't let this fool you in regards to the power of this program.

The area where the image of the Poser manikin is displayed is where your OBJ mesh will be displayed for editing. Most of the commands that you will use are in the Edit pull down menu but there are a couple that come in quite handy that are somewhat hidden. The first is Ctrl+{ (control key plus the open bracket key) which will hide any portion of the mesh highlighted on the screen or all of the mesh if nothing is selected. The other one is Ctrl+} (control key plus the close bracket key) which will display any hidden portions of the mesh that are selected or all of the mesh if nothing is selected and something is hidden.

**PHI-Builder** – Written by Roy Riggs

Sorry Suzanne, PHI-Builder is not used for giving you strong and shapely PHI's but it can take a lot of weight off your mind when trying to get a character into Poser. The interface as shown in Figure 1-3 is again simple but this program packs a punch too.

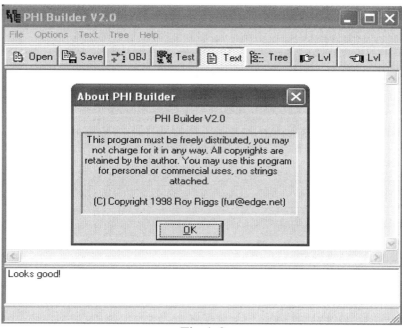

Fig 1-3

Although this program was written in 1998, it is still a valuable tool for creators of Poser character content. If used properly and all the joint presets are done right in this program, a lot of your problems setting JPs in Poser are reduced or eliminated. Back in Poser3 I used to have to write my PHI files by hand using a text program like WordPad. When Roy first released the original version of this program I felt like bowing and kissing his feet.

PHI-Builder is used to predefine joint rotation orders and the basic hierarchy of the body structure based on the named body parts of the OBJ mesh. This program is used after you have defined the body part names in UVMapper and before bringing the mesh into Poser.

**Artweaver** – Written by Boris Eyrich

Artweaver is a program that I just recently discovered but have fallen in love with. Although for most of my image work I use Adobe Photoshop, Artweaver is an excellent clone of Photoshop with nearly all the capabilities of its much more expensive big brother. Although I highly recommend Photoshop for those that can afford it, Artweaver is an excellent alternative for those who cannot. An example of the interface can be seen in Figure 1-4

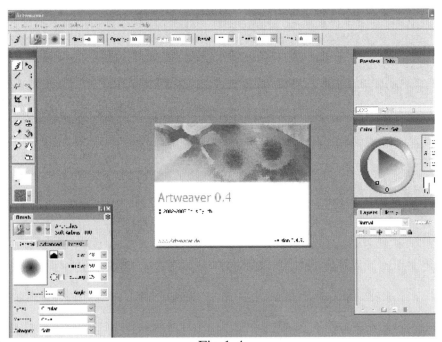

Fig 1-4

If you don't have a paint program, you may use Artweaver to paint your texture maps for use on the mesh after assigning material zones to the mesh in UVMapper and creating your UV Maps for painting.

**Poser** – Written by eFrontier/Smith Micro

I am including a shot of of the Poser interface here for reference only, Figure 1-5. If you don't know what Poser is, or what it looks like, you are reading the wrong book. This is obviously where you want your characters to end up so you can pose them, animate them, render them, and share your image and animations with all your family and friends. Hopefully I will do my job properly and by then end of this book you will be able to do this with a character you rigged and textured yourself.

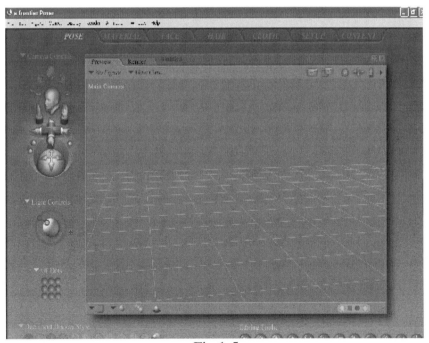

Fig 1-5

## Chapter 2: Frankenstein 101

You may ask me, why is this chapter called Frankenstein 101? Well, we are going to cut a person up, drag their body parts all over the scream ... er screen ... attach names to the various dismembered parts then dump them into a file. That file we are going to load into another program that we will use to jab sticks with hinges and balls attached to them into the body parts so that when we finally suck the tattered remains into Poser, it will be reborn again as a fully functioning human.

Well, almost.

Now, have you downloaded the Free content from my portfolio on the Internet that we will be using? What? NO? Well what are you waiting for?

I'm going to get some coffee while you do that.

Got it now? Good! Let's take a look at what is in the archive.

Hmmm, don't need that yet, or that, but what do we have here ... BoxMan.obj. Let's drag him out and give him some simple arm and leg joints, shall we?

I will assume you know how to copy and paste files from one location to another and how to create new folders. If you don't, we are in serious trouble.

So here is what you do:

1 – Create a new folder in your Poser runtime in the Characters folder (poser/runtime/libraries/character) called BoxMan.

2 - Copy the Boxman.obj to the Boxman folder.

Note: The archive creates a runtime folder identical to your Poser structure so by copying the runtime created into the Poser runtime, all the content and folders will be created for you.

Now start UVMapper Classic ... what? You haven't installed the programs? What are you waiting for? Get them installed ... NOW!

I'll sit here tapping my finger impatiently while I wait.

Now let's start UVMapper Classic and load the BoxMan.obj.

After starting UVMapper, use the File drop down menu to select Load Model and navigate to the directory in your runtime where you placed the obj. Click on BoxMan.obj and load the model. Your screen should look something like Figure 2-1.

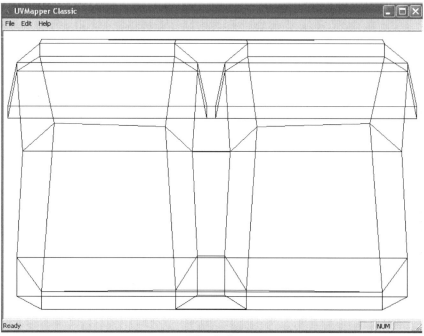

Fig 2-1

That doesn't look much like an animation character does it? Well, we need to do a little work before it looks right in UVMapper. At this point there is no need to select any portion of the model. Just click the Edit drop down menu and navigate to the New UV Map pop-out menu and select Planar from the listed choices. See Figure 2–2.

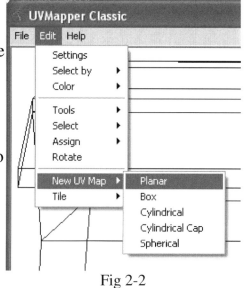

Fig 2-2

This will provide a dialog box like the one pictured in Figure 2–3. On this dialog box click the radio buttons for Z-Axis in Alignment and Don't Split in the Split area as indicated. Click the OK button.

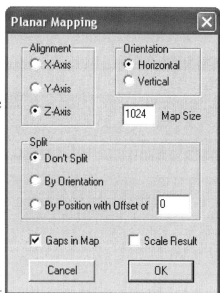

This will provide you with a view of the model with the UVs organized as a front view as seen in Figure 2–4.

Fig 2-3

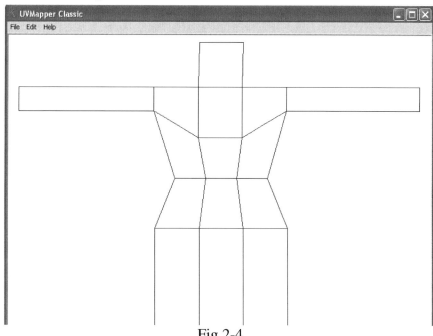

Fig 2-4

Say hello to BoxMan. He looks a little bit better now. But now we need to dismember him. We'll start by cutting off his arms.

Selecting parts of a mesh in UVMapper is as easy as left clicking the mouse button and dragging a selection box over the polygons you want to select. See Figure 2-5

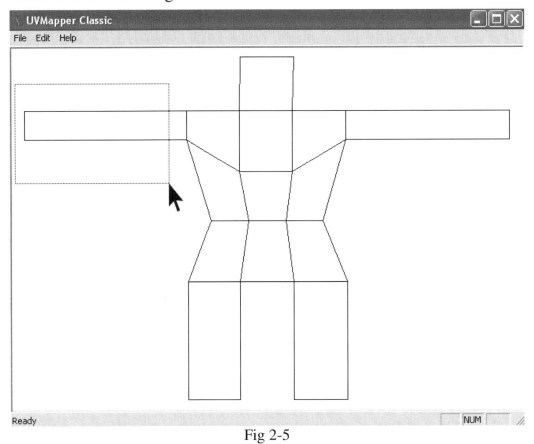

Fig 2-5

After selecting the area of the mesh you want to work on, release the left mouse button and the selection area becomes a bounding box with 8 resizing handles and the selected portion of the mesh turns red and becomes dotted lines. See Figure 2-6 (trust me, the selected item is red).

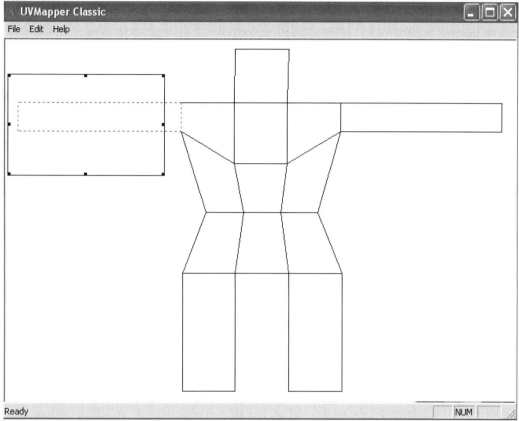

Fig 2-6

Once you have selected the polygons you want to name, go back to the Edit drop down menu and from the Assign pop-out menu select to Group as shown in Figure 2-7.

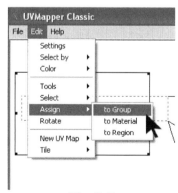

Fig 2-7

You will now have a dialog display with a drop down text box as shown in Figure 2-8.

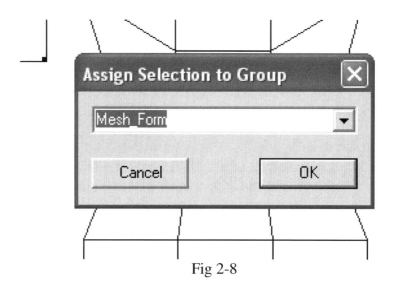

Fig 2-8

In the space with the highlighted words Mesh_Form (it could say something else too) type in the name of the body part. In this case we'll use the name rArm, for right arm, and then click OK. You will then be presented with another dialog box saying you are creating a new group. Accept this notice by clicking Yes.

Congratulations you have just named your first body part.

While the body part is still selected, press the key combination Ctrl+{ to make the body part invisible so that you cannot accidentally select it again.

Repeat the above process to select and name the left arm. Use the name lArm to name it and then make it invisible too.

Repeat again to select first the right leg and name it rLeg and make it invisible. Do the same for the left leg naming it lLeg and make it invisible.

Why make the body parts invisible as I select them? You may ask. Well, as stated above the simple reason is so that you don't accidentally reselect them and add them to another body part. Another reason is that as you hide them you can visually see what is left that needs to be named. Since the arms and legs are now invisible, we can easily select the remaining three body parts.

First select the head and name it head. Then make it invisible. Second select the chest area down to just above the waist line and name it chest. Then make it invisible (See how making the arms and head invisible made selecting the chest easier?) Third select the final body part and name it hip. No need to make it invisible, but click anywhere in UVMapper window to deselect it.

Now all the body parts for BoxMan have been named. Click the key combination Ctrl+} to make all the parts visible again.

From the drop down menu select File and Save the model to the Boxman folder with a name like: Boxman2.OBJ. For our purposes just accept the default options on the save screen as shown in Fig 2-9. This will preserve your original file so that if you ever need to go back to it, you still have it.

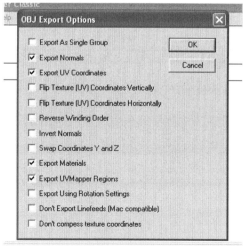

Fig 2-9

## Chapter 3: If Phi were King

Now that we have named all the body parts for BoxMan by cutting him apart, we need to find a way to tell Poser what to do with those parts. Many of you are probably familiar with the CR2 file that is used to control the parts of an OBJ mesh so that it can be posed. Where the OBJ is like a corpse waiting to be animated, the CR2 is like all the internal organs, brains, and bones that make the body live and breath.

But how is the CR2 created? Well, if you look at one in a text editor like Wordpad, you will see it is, strictly speaking, a text file. You will even see many words and references in the file that you will recognize and know to some degree what they might mean. In fact, if one wanted to, you could even write a CR2 from scratch and conceivably get an OBJ to come to life in Poser. This is not the recommended way to do it. You can also import the OBJ into Poser and take it into the Setup room (P4Pro, P5, P6 and now P7 support this) but for the beginner this can be a daunting task and potentially be very confusing.

So is there an easy way to create a CR2? The short answer is YES and it is called the PHI file. I don't ever remember seeing a break out of the acronym PHI but my way of thinking has always broken it out to mean Poser Hierarchy Instructions file. When this file is imported into Poser it will find the associated OBJ and automatically create the CR2 for you. There are pit falls to this process and if you are not careful in how you set up the PHI file, it can result in a mess in Poser or a total failure of creating the character CR2 altogether. That is why the program PHI-Builder was written by Roy Riggs and that is why it is such a help to new Poser character creators. It'll let you create a faulty PHI file, but it usually tells you that it's faulty.

Now let's start PHI-Builder and put the bones, organs, and brains into BoxMan so he can live in Poser.

As shown in Chapter 1 and again here in Figure 3-1, the PHI-Builder interface is fairly simple.

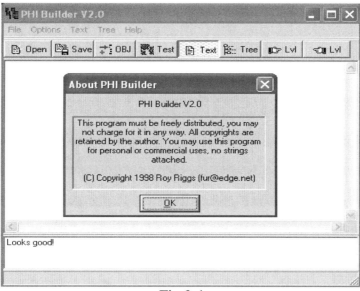

Fig 3-1

But it can also cause a little confusion. Most people would immediately try to use the Open command from the icon menu to start working. WRONG! Open and Save are used to either bring in a PHI file to be worked on or to save one out to a file. The first thing we want to do is import an OBJ into PHI-Builder and that is done using the OBJ Icon right next to the save Icon. Clicking on the OBJ Icon will open the Open dialog box for importing an OBJ as seen in Fig 3-2. For ease of use it is a good idea to use the program in the TREE mode. So after loading the OBJ click the Tree Icon to set this mode.

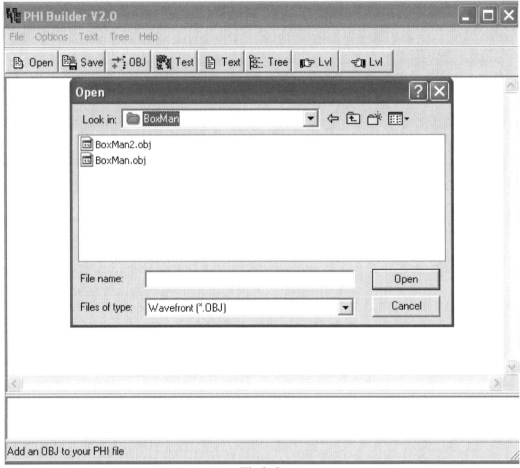

Fig3-2

PHI-Builder will default to the Geometry folder of your Poser install but since we put the OBJ for BoxMan in the the BoxMan folder in the Character library of the runtime, we need to navigate to that location and load the OBJ we created with UVMapper called BoxMan2.OBJ as shown in Figure 3-2. Click on BoxMan2.OBJ to select it and then click open to load it into PHI-Builder. You should now have a screen that looks like Figure 3-3.

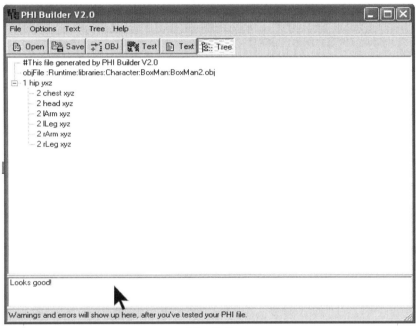
Fig 3-3

If you look at the text area where the cursor is pointing you'll see it says "Looks good!". Below that area is a message box that tells you that "Warnings and errors will show up here, after you've tested your PHI file". Now click on the Test Icon next to the OBJ Icon in the menu bar. The text box at the bottom will still say "Looks good!". And even though this PHI file would load BoxMan into Poser and create a CR2, the rotation order of 4 of the 7 joints is incorrect and so is the hierarchy.

Look closely at the rotation order of the following joints as indicated by the three letters after the joint name: head, chest, rLeg, and lLeg. Now remember that we discussed in Chapter 1 that the first rotation on all joints should be the Twist rotation or the Axis that runs through the body part. Let's look at a picture of BoxMan and see what those rotations should be in Figure 3-4.

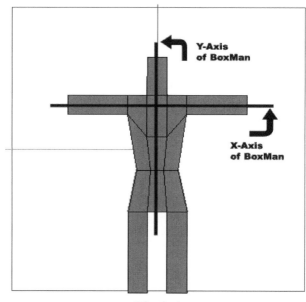

Fig 3-4

As you can see in the picture, the X Axis runs through the arms from right to left so the orientation applied in PHI-Builder is correct for the Twist rotation. But the Y Axis runs through the rest of the body parts from top to bottom so the X Axis applied by PHI-Builder is incorrect. But before we fix this, let's look at what the other two rotations should be after the X Twist for the arms and Y Twist for the other body parts. The best way to think of the order of rotation is as an ascending priority of movement. Since the Twist movement is the most restricted the one after that would be the average restricted movement and the last one would be the least restricted movement for the joint.

So let's look at the arm rotations that PHI-Builder applied and see how they associate with joint restrictions.

PHI-Builder assigned a rotation order of XYZ to the arms. We know that X is the most restricted so it is fine as the first rotation. The Y rotation would be the motion of the arm moving forward and backwards from a position at 90 degrees from the body. Moving forward the arm has a movement of about 100 to 110 degrees. Moving backwards it has approximately 20 degrees. The Z Axis represents the arm moving up and down from the 90 degree position. In this movement the arm can move down about 90 to 100 degrees and up about the same amount. So from this comparison it would appear that the rotation of XYZ would be appropriate for the arm of BoxMan.

For the remainder of the body joints of BoxMan, the X rotation representing a forward and backward movement or bending that would be the least restrictive. Moving from side to side is against the natural movement of the joint. So a rotation of YZX would be the most appropriate for these joints.

So we need to change the rotation of the joints for the head, chest, and both legs to YZX instead of XYZ. To do this, double click on the joint to activate a popup box that will have dot markers for all the available rotations for the joint as shown in Figure 3-5.

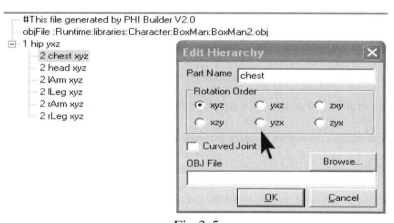

Fig 3-5

After changing the rotation to YZX, click OK to save the change and then proceed to the other joints that need to be changed and do the same for them.

There is one more item we need to look at before we are done with PHI-Builder, as mentioned above, and that is the hierarchy of the body parts. If you look at the association as assigned by PHI-Builder in Figure 3-6 you will note that there are only two levels of grouping. All the body parts are spawning off of the hip.

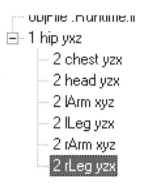

Fig 3-6

Although it is fine for the legs and chest to spawn off of the hip, the arms and head spawn off of the chest. So we need to associate the head and arms as being sub-parts to the chest and not the hip. To do this, click on the parts one at a time and drag them on top of the chest body part. You will see the associating dotted line change from connecting them to the hip to the chest and their hierarchy number will change to a level 3 instead of level 2 as shown in in Figure 3-7.

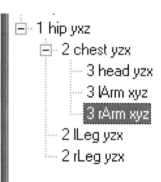

Fig 3-7

OK, if we did everything correctly as described above we can now save the file. Click on the Save icon in the menu bar. On the presented dialog box enter the name of the OBJ file you originally loaded, BoxMan2, in the text area provided for the file name and click Save.

The PHI file has now been created. Now let's find out if we did it correctly.

Start your Poser software. When you get to the main screen, click File in the drop down menu and look about ¾ of the way down on the menu you'll see: Convert Hier File... (Figure 3-8) Click this command to bring up the navigation dialog box for opening a Hierarchy file. Poser will default to the Poser install directory so just click Runtime, libraries, Character, BoxMan to get to where you need to be. You will see the BoxMan2.PHI file displayed there. Select it and click Open. A small dialog box with a single text entry area will appear and Poser will prompt you to enter a name for your new character. Enter the name BoxMan and click OK.

Fig 3-8

Congratulations, if everything went well, you have just created your first Poser Character.

Now let's take a look at him.

In the Poser figures library navigate to your folder for BoxMan and open it. OOPS, where's BoxMan? Never fear, Poser saves all new characters created using PHI files to the New Figures folder and not the folder of origin. Back out of the BoxMan folder and open the New Figures folder and at or near the top should be a file named BoxMan. (Figure 3-9) At this point it will have a blank image thumbnail. Click on the thumbnail for BoxMan to load your character. You should now have BoxMan living and breathing in Poser as shown in Figure 3-10.

Fig 3-9

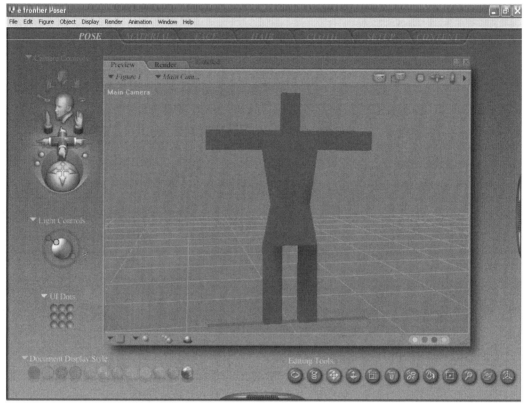
Fig 3-10

Go ahead and play with him. Posing is limited because of the small number of joints and the joints may do some funky things, but we haven't even scratched the surface of what can be done to refine a character's movement. That will be explained in a later chapter.

Now navigate back to the BoxMan figure folder and save a copy of your character there for future use. If you want to share your creation with a friend, just Zip the BoxMan folder in the Character library and give it to them. Everything you need to make BoxMan work is in that one folder instead of scattered around your Runtime.

## Chapter 4: Project 1
### She Can Dance

Remember the age of Disco? I remember my first day of senior high school. I showed up wearing a cranberry colored crushed velvet leisure suit, a paisley print silk shirt, pooka beads choker necklace, and white patten leather dance boots. All the girls wanted to date me because I looked like John Travolta and all the guys wanted to beat my ass because I looked too cool. Nowadays if I dressed that way, the girls would want to beat my ass and the guys would want to date me. Go figure.

My point in relation to Poser? None whatsoever. But we are going to have a girl dancing in Poser by the end of this chapter if all goes well.

OK, now in the Poser/Runtime/libraries/Character folder create a new folder called FemProj1. After creating this folder copy the FemProj1.OBJ from where you stored the resource files to this folder.

## Part 1: UV Mapper

The first step, same as it was for BoxMan, is to get the character broken down into the basic body parts and name them for use in Poser. So start UVMapper and load the FemPro1.OBJ into the program. You should have a screen similar to one in Figure 4-1 if all is well.

Fig 4-1

That doesn't look much like a woman let alone someone who could dance. But, like BoxMan, the UV coordinates are all screwed up right now. So let's fix them so we can see what we are doing. From the drop down menu select Edit, New UV Map, and then Planar from the Pop-Out menu. As before select Z Axis alignment and Don't Split for splitting. Click OK and the screen should look more like Figure 4-2.

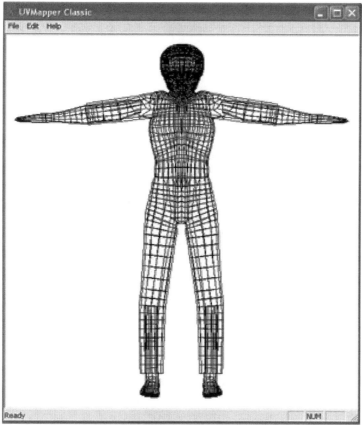
Fig 4-2

This looks a lot better. At least it looks human and it even looks a little like a woman. Don't let the more dense mesh scare you. This character is still what is considered low poly. It can get FAR worse as you get involved in more and more complex models. But that is for a different book. Right now we have to look at how we are going to cut this pretty little lady up so we can bone her. That sounds like something out of a Rob Zombie movie.

First let's look at how many joints we need to make this character move properly. For a basic character you need joints at the following locations: head and neck, two in the torso, three for each leg and three for each arm. How many is that? What do mean you didn't keep count? Well, it's a total of 19.

What do you mean you count 16?

It's 19, trust me. In Poser 1+1+2+3+3+3+3=19.

What do you mean you still only count 16?

Well, it's 19 ... because I'm the teacher and you're not!

Now let me show you how the joints break down. In Figure 4-3 you will see how we are going to dismember this poor girl.

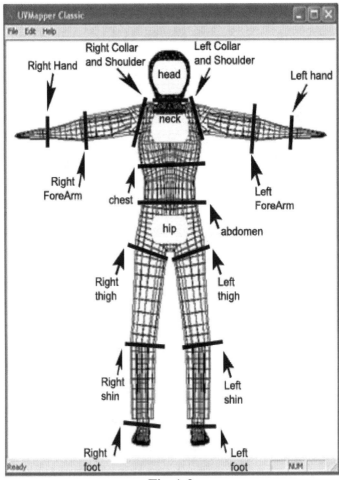

Fig 4-3

OK, I admit it, it was a trick question. The shoulder joints are a combination of two joints working together and the hip is a fixed joint. That's where the 3 extra joints come from to make a total of 19. Although technically the shoulder is a single joint, because of the way it moves and the extremes of position it can achieve, Poser breaks it down into two joints to allow better mesh blending at extreme poses. The hip, while not technically a joint, is the center of the Poser universe and as such is the rotation point that all the other body parts center on and spawn out from. In Italy, all roads lead back to Rome. In Poser, all joints lead back to the hip.

Although in Poser the body parts can be named anything, there are some naming conventions that are considered to be standards that most people use as follows: head, neck, chest, abdomen, hip, rThigh, lThigh, rShin, lShin, rFoot, lFoot, rCollar, lCollar, rShldr, lShldr, rForeArm, lForeArm, rHand, lHand.

Note the way capitals and lower case letters are used when naming a body part? In Poser if these naming conventions are followed, Poser will automatically assign full names to the body parts when selected in Poser for posing.

So with the breakdown of the body parts as shown in Figure 4-3 and names identified above, let's start cutting up our tiny dancer so she can boogie down at the end of the chapter.

As with BoxMan we will start with the outer most appendages and work our way in to the larger and more complex ones. The first to get cut off and named should be either the right or left hand. I'm right handed so I always start with the right hand.

As described in Chapter 2, drag a selection box over the right hand to a point just below what would be considered the wrist as shown in Figure 4-4.

While the right hand is highlighted by the bounding box with 8 resizing handles, select Edit from the drop down menu and select Assign > to Group and then enter rHand in the text box presented and click OK. Click yes to accept the naming of the new group.

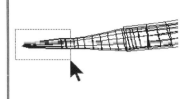

Fig 4-4

Now be sure to click Ctrl+{ to make the hand invisible so that you don't accidentally include it, or part of it, in any other body parts.

Now go ahead and name the rest of the arm parts for the left and right arms as shown in the picture sequence in Figure 4-5.

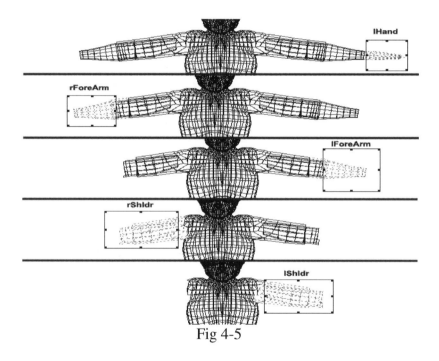

Fig 4-5

We won't be selecting and naming the secondary part of the shoulder joints (the collar joints) right now because it would be a little bit difficult to accurately define them. We'll wait a little bit and I'll show you an easy way to do it without hurting the tiny dancer ... too much. Now be sure that as you name each body part for the arms, you do the

Ctrl+{ key combination to make the body part invisible. This is also a good way to visually identify what parts you have named and what still needs to be cut off and named.

Now let's move down to her legs. Use Figure 4-5 as a reference as to how to define and name the parts of the legs.

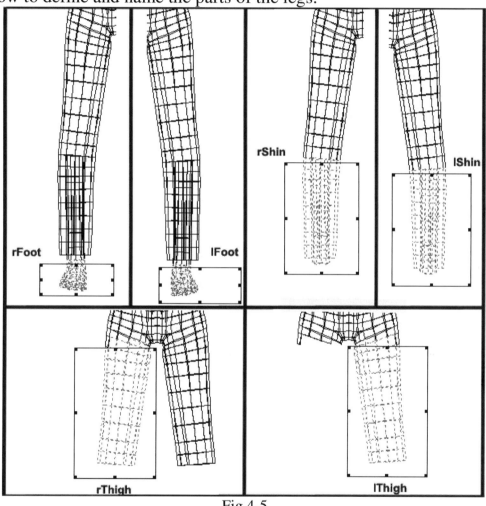

Fig 4-5

Again, be sure that as you name each body part for the legs, you do the Ctrl+{ key combination to make the body part invisible.

You should now have a great deal of unused space surrounding what is left of the mesh on the screen. Let's use this space to our advantage.

Move the mouse cursor into the upper right hand corner of the mesh display box, right click and drag down to the bottom left corner selecting the remaining portions of the mesh in a very large selection box. From the menu select Edit > New UV Map > Planar. In the dialog box the selection should still be zAxis and Don't Split. If not, select these options again and click OK. The remaining portion of the mesh should now be filling the screen. Now go into the drop down menu for Edit again and click Select > None to clear the mesh from being selected.

Does she look like she has a sad look on her face? Well, considering she just had her arms and legs cut off, she probably feels like a character in the movie SAW-IV. Ouch!

If you look at the areas around the left shoulder and the hip where the right and left leg attach, Figure 4-6, you'll notice that the poly edges there are a little ragged.

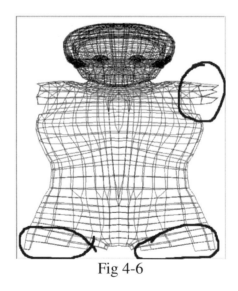

Fig 4-6

Note: Your accuracy may have been better and actually included the polygons on the left shoulder. If it did, kudos to you. But there is no way to get all the polygons for either thigh with a single drag of the mouse.

Although we could leave joint edges like this for this project, let's go ahead and clean them up so that the right and left side shoulder joints match and she has a nice clean bikini line.

The selection and naming of the polygons on the left shoulder is as simple as dragging a selection box over the polygons and then going into the Edit menu, selecting Assign > to Group and then using the drop-down scroll bar to find lShldr, clicking it and then clicking OK.

Be sure to make those polys invisible now.

The thigh groups are going to be a little bit more difficult and will require at least two selections for each side. Take a look at Figure 4-7 for how the right thigh is fixed.

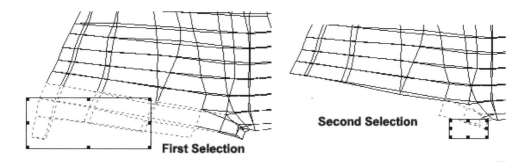

Fig 4-7

After selecting and adding these polys to the rThigh in the same way we added the polys to the lShldr, go ahead and make them invisible so that they cannot be selected again by accident. Then go ahead and do the same thing for the left thigh. When completed, the area should look like Figure 4-8.

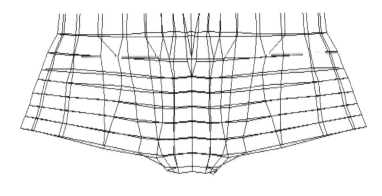

Fig 4-8

Now we have a nice clean bikini line with no waxing required.

Let's fire up the chainsaw and go after the rest of the torso, shall we?

Select the hip as shown in Figure 4-9. Name it and make it invisible.

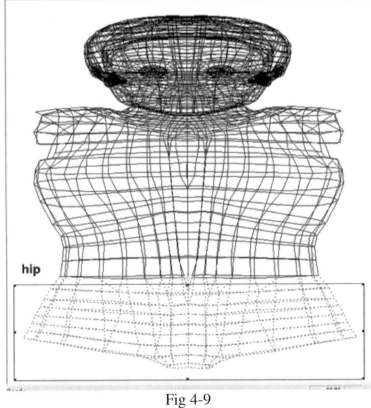

Fig 4-9

Now let's grab the abdomen as shown in Figure 4-10. But it looks like we might not have gotten all of the abdomen's polygons so we'll probably have to do a second selection after naming the first one.

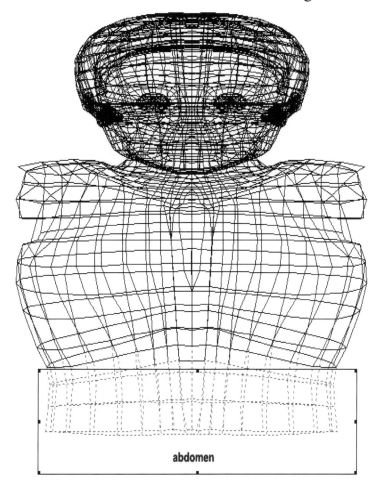

Fig 4-10

If you look at Figure 4-11 you'll see that the middle section of the abdomen was missed in the first selection. Just select the remaining polys as shown here and add them to the abdomen group as explained above.

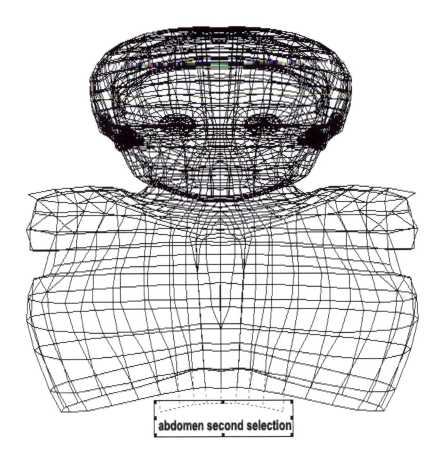

Fig 4-11

Now all that's left is her upper body, neck, and head, let's resize what's left of her so we can see what we are doing a little better again. As before, right click the mouse cursor in the upper right hand corner of the display area and drag a selection box down to the left hand bottom corner. From the Edit menu select New UV Map > Planar. The Z-Axis/Don't Split should still be selected so Click OK to resize the image.

Now you can more easily see the polygons in the right and left shoulder for selecting to name the collar portion of the shoulder joints. Go ahead and select and name the areas for the rCollar and lCollar as shown in Figure 4-12. Many people will include much more of the breast area in the selection for the collars but that is not needed for this character.

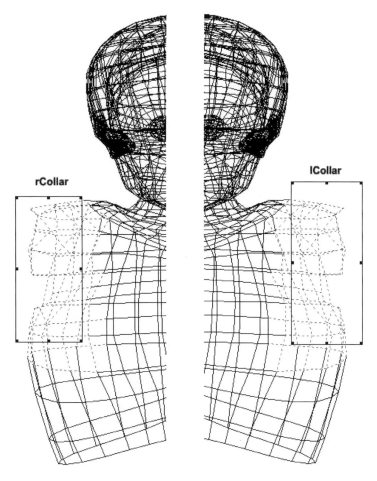

Fig 4-12

After naming each one, be sure to make them invisible so that they don't accidentally get included with the next mesh grouping.

Now we are ready to attack her chest!

Because of the close proximity of the neck and the way the inner most part of her shoulders rise up, this will take several cuts as shown in the following image sequences in Figure 4-13.

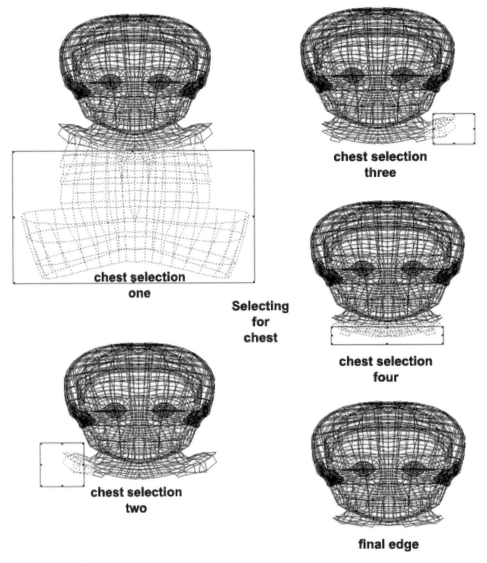

Fig 4-13

With all of those parts of the chest selected and added together and hidden, all we have left is the neck and head. These were saved for last because to accurately separate the neck from the head, you need to look at the mesh from a different angle. Drag a selection box that is slightly larger than the head and neck to highlight them. From the menu select Edit > New UV Map > Planar. In the dialog box we still want to not split the mesh, so leave Don't Split selected. But for the Alignment we want to change that to the X-Axis so that we are looking at the mesh from the side as shown in Figure 4-14.

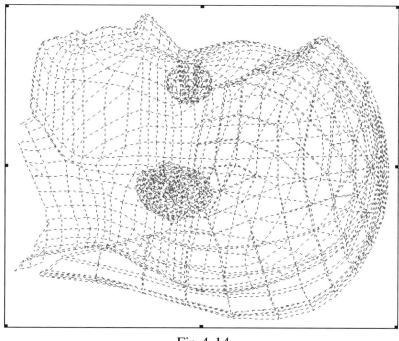
Fig 4-14

As you can see on the bottom of the neck we have a couple of problems. At the base of the neck in the back there are some polygons that are part of the chest and at the front of the neck there are some polygons missing that were added into the chest by mistake. Let's go ahead and fix the ones at the back of the neck now but the missing ones will have to wait until later.

Go ahead and select the polygons at the base of the neck as shown in Fig 4-15 and add them into the chest through the Edit >Assign > to Group commands in the Edit menu.

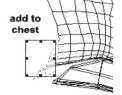

Fig 4-15

OK, now we can go for the jugular. But because of the way the neck is positioned under the head we'll have to select it in two parts as shown in Figure 4-16.

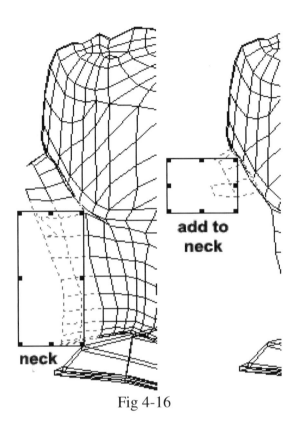

Fig 4-16

After selecting and adding both these parts to the neck group, be sure to make them invisible like all the previous parts.

Now drag a selection box around the head and assign it to the head group using the Edit > Assign > to Group command from the Edit menu. Then make the head invisible too.

Now we need to do a quick fix on those missing neck polygons that got added to the chest by accident. Since everything is invisible, go into the Edit menu and click the Select command and then select By Group. From the list presented, click chest. On the screen you will have a selection box displayed but it will be empty. Now we can use the Ctrl+} key combination to make the chest parts visible. You should now have a display similar to the one in Figure 4-17.

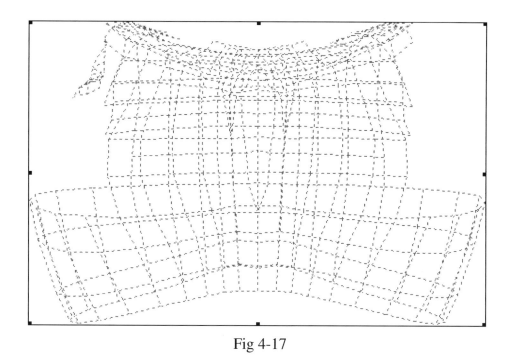

Fig 4-17

The easiest way to fix the missing neck polygons is to select the upper middle portion of the chest as shown in Figure 4-18.

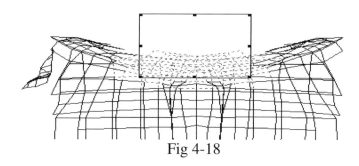

Fig 4-18

While this section is selected, switch the view to the X-Axis by using the Edit > New UV Map > Planar command and setting the

Alignment to X-Axis and the Split to Don't Split (which it should already be at from changing the view of the head and neck). Your view will look like Figure 4-19 and you can easily select the missing polygons as shown and add them to the neck using the Edit > Assign > to Group command.

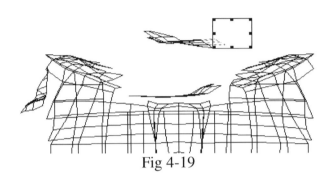

Fig 4-19

We are now finished naming all the body parts for the Tiny Dancer. But before we save the file, let's make all the body parts visible. Click any where in the display area to turn off any selected areas and then click Ctrl+} to make the invisible items visible again. Looks like a mess doesn't it? But don't worry, we haven't changed the mesh at all, just the way the UVs line up in a 2D image. Later on when we start working on setting up a UV Map, all of these items will be rearranged so that they make a lot more sense on the screen. But for now we don't need to worry about that.

So now, from the menu, select File > Save Model. In the next dialog box click OK to accept the default settings and then in the Save dialog box, type TinyDancer in the text area provided for naming the file. Click OK to save.

We are finished using UVMapper for this project so go ahead and shut it down.

It's time to move on to the next program: PHI-Builder.

## Part 2: PHI-Builder

OK, let's fire up PHI-Builder and see if we can build up the Tiny Dancer's PHIs!

Remember to click OBJ to load the mesh and navigate to where you saved the TinyDancer.OBJ. It should be: Poser/Runtime/libraries/Character/FemProj1/ just in case you forgot. But of course you may have been disagreeable and placed it somewhere else. Shame on you!

When the mesh is loaded you should have a screen that looks similar to the one in Figure 4-20.

Fig 4-20

Now even though PHI-Builder says 'Looks Good', let's look at what it created.

The abdomen is attached to the hip – good. The chest is attached to the abdomen – good. The head is attached to the abdomen? The lCollar, lFoot, and lHand are attached to abdomen? And we even have the lForeArm attached to lFoot. No need to go any further, if this creature got loose it would look like The Thing From Another World trying to transform from a dog into a human. Not a pretty sight and not very conducive to dancing.

Obviously we need to do some work on the hierarchy before we do anything else.

So let's start dragging her body parts around. While you do this you can hum the leg-bone song if you want.

The leg bones connected to the hip bone. The head bones connected to the neck bone. The collar bones are connected to the chest bone ... and hear the word of the ME!

Take a look at Figure 4-21 if you're unsure what body parts should attach to what body parts. Although it really worries me if you can't figure that out by looking at your own body.

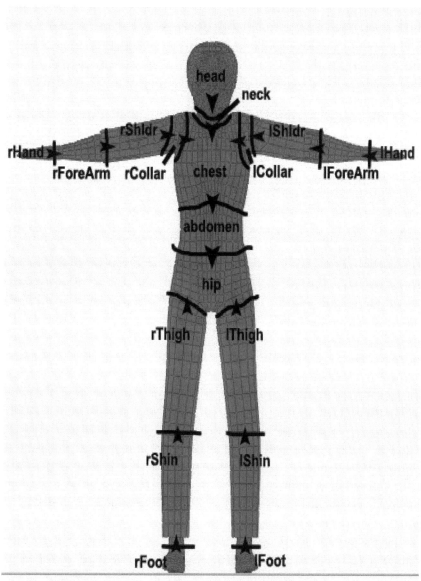

Fig 4-21

As mentioned before and illustrated above, the hip is the center of the Poser Universe with all the body parts and joints tracing back to it. Kind of like the real world where everything human springs from the hips area ... heck, most men are controlled by that area and most women are drawn to it ... but I digress. So, at the top of the Poser hierarchy is the hip with all joints spawning out from it as shown in

Figure 4-22.

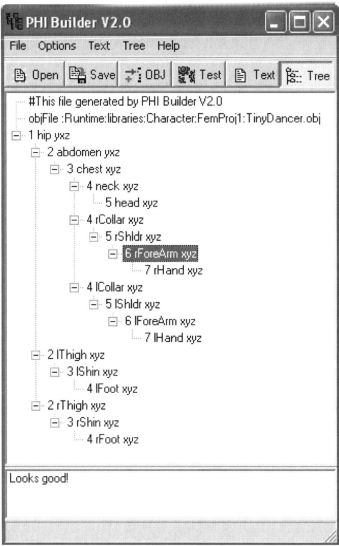

Fig 4-22

With the hierarchy fixed, let's look at the joint rotations assigned by PHI-Builder. The assignment of the YXZ rotation order to the hip is fine since the hip is pretty much a 'fixed' joint that all other body parts move around. While the assignment YXZ isn't bad for the abdomen, a better rotation (as explained in the previous chapter) would be YZX since the spine bends the easiest on the X Axis. This rotation would also be a a better choice for the following joints: chest, neck, head, rThigh, lThigh, rShin, lShin, rFoot, and lFoot. All of these joints Twist on the Y Axis and Bend on the X Axis. The Z Axis has a limited movement for all of these from side to side. So go ahead and change the rotation order for these joints to YZX.

You don't remember how? I should slap you. Double click on the joint name to open up the dialog box with the joint rotation orders listed for the joint and highlight the dot next to the rotation order you want to use and then click OK. Your rotation orders should now look like the ones shown in Figure 4-23.

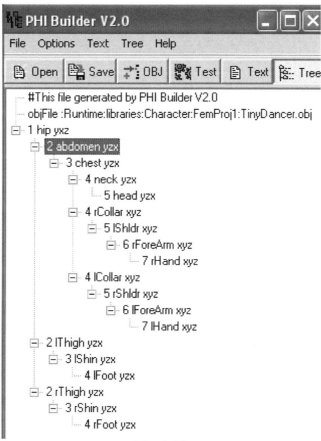

Fig 4-23

Now let's look at the remaining rotations for the arms. The rotations assigned by PHI-Builder for the collar, shldr, and hand for both right and left look good with the XYZ. But let's consider the forearm rotation set to XYZ. Although this is OK for use in Poser. A better choice would be XZY. To illustrate this, put your arm out at your side at 90 degrees with your palm down. We have already shown that the elbow (forearm joint) Twists on the X Axis which runs through the arm from left to right. The direction the joint moves the easiest is forward. In fact you can bend your arm at the elbow to the point where your hand touches your chest. Not HER chest, your chest ... behave yourself. If you try to move your arm from side to side (or up and down) at the elbow, you might be able to move it 1 or 2 degrees but it is forcing the joint to move in an unnatural way. So the Twist and Bend are X and Y with Z in the middle as the Side to Side movement. Go ahead and change the rotation for the right and left forearm to XZY.

OK, are we done with PHI-Builder? Well, yes and no. While you can save the PHI file and use it at this point to create the character in Poser, there is one more thing we can do with PHI-Builder that will make the character a little more controllable in Poser. We can add IK to the legs.

What's IK you ask? It's like dropping your brain into your feet. IK stands for Inverse Kinematics. A real world version of IK is the old snake toy where you hold the end of the snakes tail and when you twist the tail the snake bobs around and bends along the body up to the head (Figure 4-24). That's IK, you are controlling the head from the tail. In this case, by putting IK on the legs, you end up controlling the movement of the legs by dragging the feet around. Although this may sound strange, it is needed to get the legs to work properly for walking and ... DANCING!

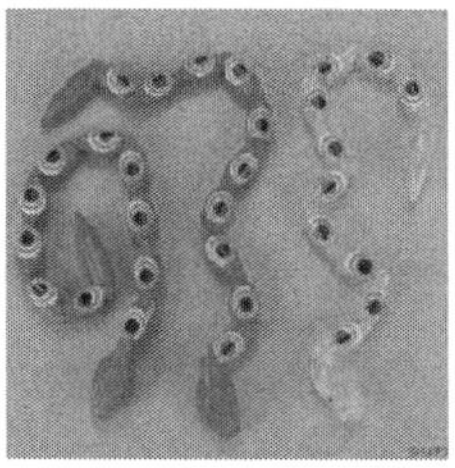

Fig 4-24

So now you ask, "How do we do IK?"

Glad you asked.

If you click on the Tree menu option in the text menu bar above the icon menu bar, you will see a drop down menu that includes the command "Add IK Chain". Click on this command to activate the dialog box for creating an IK chain. (Figure 4-25)

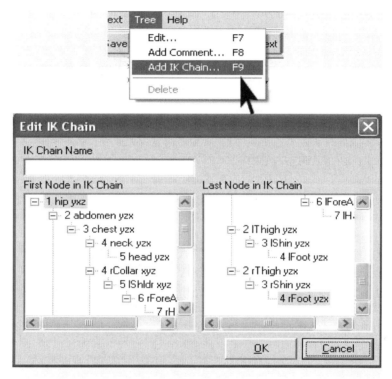

Fig 4-25

Make sure you have the hip joint highlighted when activating this as PHI-Building will attempt to create an IK chain based off of whatever joint you have highlighted. On the Edit IK Chain screen you want to enter the name of the IK chain you are creating, in this case either the RightLeg or the LeftLeg (note: there is no space in the name for the IK chain) needs to be typed in the IK Chain Name text box. In the display box to the left scroll down to the first joint of the IK Chain you want to create. If it is the RightLeg, the first joint will be the rThigh. In the display box to the right, scroll down to the last joint of the IK Chain you want to create. If it is the RightLeg, select rFoot.

Now click OK and PHI-Builder will create the chain for you. Do this for both the right and left. Your screen should now look like Figure 4-26.

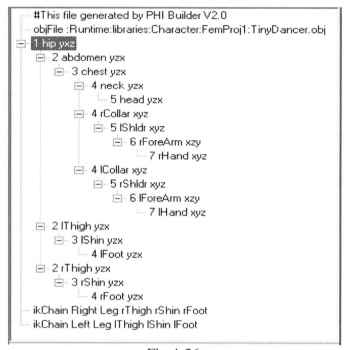

Fig 4-26

Although you could create an IK chain for each arm that would include the collar joint down through the hand, it is not really needed for this character.

We can now save the PHI file using the Save icon in the menu bar. Click the icon and enter the name TinyDancer for your file name.

OK, if everything has worked the way it's supposed to, we now have a functional PHI file for creating the character in Poser. Time to move on to step 3.

## Step 3: Poser

We are now ready to bring the Tiny Dancer to life in Poser. Go ahead and load your copy of Poser. On the main screen select File from the drop down menu and click Convert Hier File ...

Now navigate to your runtime folder FemProj1 to find the PHI file we just created. When you locate the tinydancer.PHI file, click it and select Open. In the text box presented for New Figure File Name: enter TinyDancer and click OK.

Congratulation you just created your second Poser character. Now let's have a look at her.

Now remember, new characters created this way default to the New Figures library in the Poser folders. So go the the New Figures library, locate the new Tiny Dancer character and load her into Poser.

If all is well, your new character should now be standing in the middle of your screen as shown in Figure 4-27.

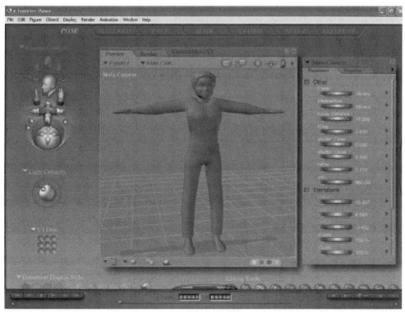

Fig 4-27

A few issues you may run into that may make you panic are:

1 - The character is absolutely HUGE. If this happens it is because of the way Poser scales OBJs versus the way other programs save them. By selecting the Body in Poser, you can usually fix this by scaling the body to 1 percent of the original size. After doing this you will want to go into the Edit > Memorize > Figure popout menu to make sure the new size is retained when saving the character back to the library.

2 - Parts of the body are oddly dark or look like they are inside out. This is caused by some of the normals being reversed so that you are seeing the inside of the body part instead of the outside. If it affects a full body part, this can be fixed by selecting the body part, going into the Grouping Tool and clicking Reverse Group Normals. If it only affects a portion of the body part, it can be fixed but that goes beyond the scope of this part of the book. So live with it!

Now let's see if she can dance. In your Pose library you should now have a folder marked Eclipse. In this folder you will find the dance files for the Tiny Dancer. Load a file onto the Tiny Dancer character. When Poser asks if you want to add frames, click Yes. In the popup bar at the bottom of the screen for controlling animations, click the Play button and sit back and watch your Tiny Dancer dance.

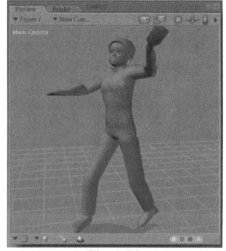

Fig 4-28

Some of the joint movement may not be prefect, but we haven't even begun looking at setting JPs. So this is a very good first step in getting a new Poser character into Poser and working properly.

## Chapter 5: Project 2
## Give Him a Hand!

In this chapter we work through setting up a human hand for use inside Poser.

Why just the hand? You may ask.

Well, the human hand is just about the most complex part of human body in terms of jointing and in the way it is used. Without the hand we could do practically nothing. You couldn't hold this book or operate your computer. Just look at your hand and count how many joints there are. One human hand has almost as many joints as the whole human body in Poser terms. So when setting up the joints for the hand, we almost have to treat each hand as a separate character that just happens to be attached to each wrist.

So let's get started.

First let's go into the Poser Runtime directory in the libraries/Characters and create a folder called HandProj2. Now copy the handproj2.OBJ from the temp directory into the folder you just created.

**Part 1: UV Mapper**

Now start up UVMapper and load the project mesh. You should have a screen that looks something like Figure 5-1.

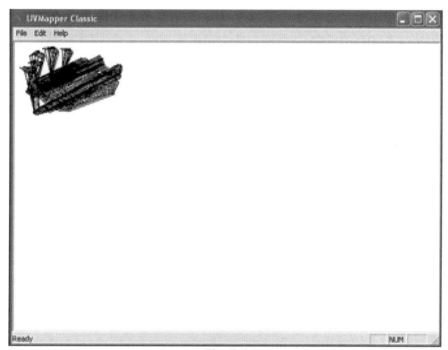
Fig 5-1

Doesn't look much like a hand does it? But then none of the other things we've loaded looked much like they were supposed to either until we looked at them correctly. Obviously we need to have the program reorder the UVs a little. And since the hand is modeled so that the palm is pointing down, it would be best if we looked at it on the Y Axis, or from above/below. So let's go into Edit > New UV

Map > Planar and in the dialog box select Y-Axis Alignment and Don't Split. Click OK and your screen should now look like Figure 5-2.

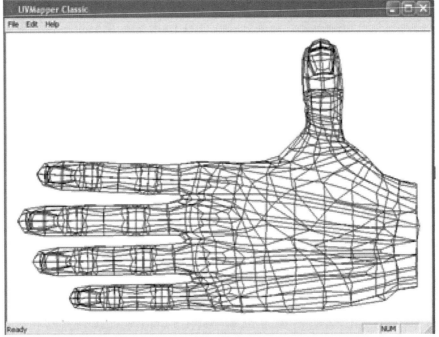

Fig 5-2

Now it looks a little bit better. If you look at the image in Figure 5-3 you'll get an idea of how to cut up the hand into it's various parts.

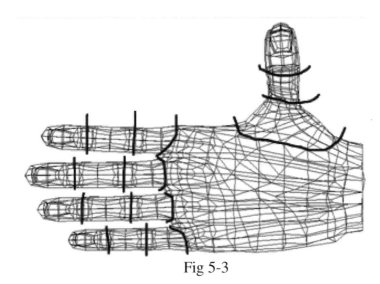

Fig 5-3

The mesh pretty much defines where to cut as each of the knuckles has a fairly obvious center to them on each of the fingers. The thumb is a little bit of a problem though and no matter what you do, it is going to be a pain to get it to work halfway right. But we'll give it a good shot.

Now let's look at the naming conventions for the various parts of the hand. Working out from the palm, which is called the hand joint, we have: Index1, Index2, Index3, Mid1, Mid2, Mid3, Ring1, Ring2, Ring2, Pinky1, Pinky2, Pinky3, Thumb1, Thumb2, and Thumb3. Of course if we were doing a right and left hand side, these names would be prefixed with an r for Right or an l for Left.

Using the image sequence in Figure 5-4, go ahead and cut up the finger joints naming them and making them invisible as you go. I'm going to step out for a cup of coffee and I'll be right back to see how you have done.

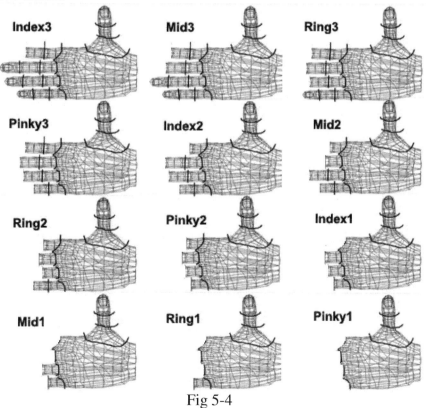

Fig 5-4

Boy, that was the best cup of coffee I've had out of a Starbuck's cup in a long time. Glad I made it and didn't buy it at Starbuck's.

Let's see how you are doing. By now you should have the hand pretty much cut down to just the palm and thumb as shown in Figure 5-5.

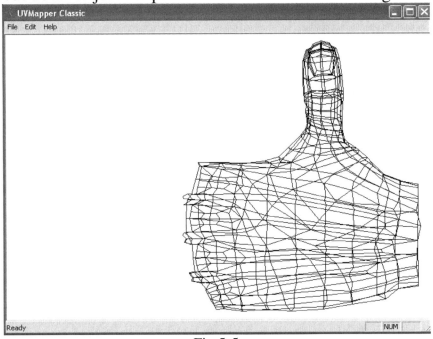
Fig 5-5

Before we cut up the thumb it is best to try and separate the thumb from the palm. You can do it the other way around but I just prefer to do it this way ... SO DO IT THIS WAY! Select groups of polys to the right of the base of the thumb and move them slightly away so that there is a space between them and the remaining polys. Then do this for a group to the left of the base of the thumb and then below the thumb until you have four groups as pictured in Figure 5-6.

What do you mean I haven't shown you how to move polys around on the screen? Oh for goodness sake, do I have to explain everything? Well, after you select a group of polys if you place the mouse cursor over the group the cursor changes to a cross with arrows pointing in all directions. Just click and hold on the group and move them where ever you want them on the screen ... preferably a place away from other polygons.

Now, look at Figure 5-6 and arrange your groups similar to this.

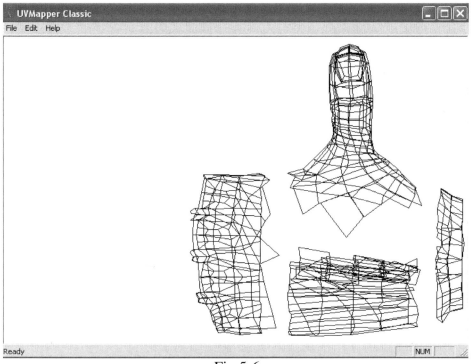

Fig 5-6

Now, one by one select the groups that make up the hand and name them hand and hide them using the Ctrl+{ key combination. When you are done doing that, drag a nice big selection box over the thumb and enlarge the view using Edit > New UV Map > Planar, making sure that the Alignment is still on the Y-Axis and the Don't Split is selected.

Your screen should now look something like Figure 5-7.

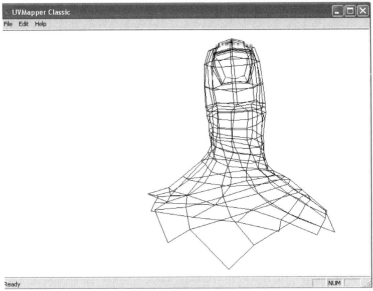
Fig 5-7

Now using the same technique we used for separating the hand into three groups, let's do the same thing for the thumb. Let's make one group for the tip, one group for the heal and leave everything else right there in the middle. Your groups should look something like Figure 5-8.

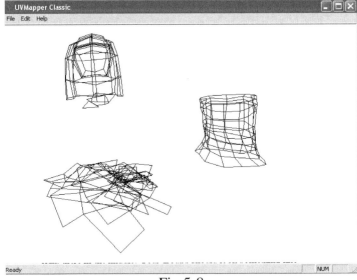
Fig 5-8

Accuracy here isn't an absolute. So don't worry if your groups are not exactly the same as pictured. Joint placement and adjustments in Poser are more important than were you cut the mesh. Now go ahead and select each of the groups one after the other and give them their proper names: thumb base = Thumb1, thumb tip = Thumb3, middle part = Thumb2.

Now go ahead and save this file back to the Poser runtime folder you created in the Characters library as: MyThing.OBJ.

Go ahead and close UVMapper.

**Part 2: PHI-Builder**

Let's start up PHI-Builder and load the OBJ for MyThing. Remember how to do that? Good. Be sure that PHI-Builder is in the Tree mode.

Your screen should look something like Figure 5-9.

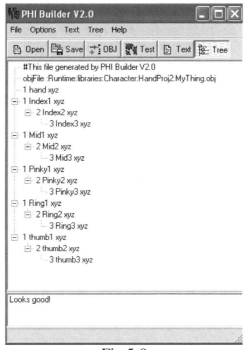

Fig 5-9

Although this file would work for bringing MyThing into Poser, there are a few issues that should be addressed first. The biggest one is the Hierarchy. As it stands right now, the fingers are not attached to the hand. All of the joints spawn off of the root as noted by the 1 in front of each of the first joint parts. To fix this, as explained in prior chapters, drag and drop the first finger segment onto the hand so that the 1 changes to a 2. If the hierarchy collapses, just click the + in front of the joint to open it back up. Now your hierarchy should look like the one shown in Figure 5-10.

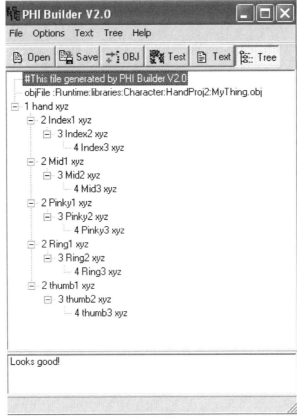

Fig 5-10

OK, that looks better. Now let's take a look at the rotation order applied by PHI-Builder. The hand and all of the finger's first rotation, or Twist, should be on the X-Axis. And it is! Great! But so is the thumb. If you look at the position of the thumb, a better rotation order for it would probably be ZYX. So let's go ahead and change that rotation order by double clicking each of the joints and highlighting the dot in front of ZYX for each joint and then clicking OK.

Your screen should now look like Figure 5-11.

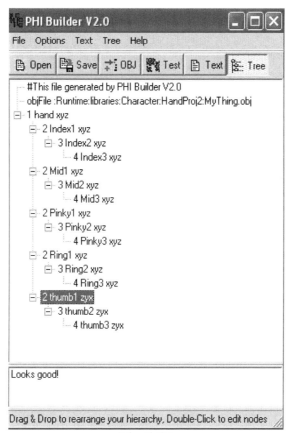
Fig 5-11

We don't need to set any IK for the hand so we are done with PHI-Builder. Go ahead and save the file and name it MyThing.PHI.

We are finished using PHI-Builder for now so go ahead and shut down the program.

**Part 3: Poser**

Now, start Poser.

When you get to the main screen, select File > Convert Heir File... from the drop down menu. Navigate to the MyThing.PHI file in the HandProj2 folder of the Characters library, select it and in the text box presented type MyThing and then click OK.

Now, go to the New Figures folder and find your new creation and load it into Poser to have a look at it.

Just for fun, set the finger joints to the following settings:

Index1 = 85 degrees on the zRotate
Mid1 = 85 degrees on the zRotate
Ring1 = 85 degrees on the zRotate
Pinky1 = 85 degrees on the zRotate

Index2 = 85 degrees on the zRotate
Mid2 = 85 degrees on the zRotate
Ring2 = 85 degrees on the zRotate
Pinky2 = 85 degrees on the zRotate

Index3 = 85 degrees on the zRotate
Mid3 = 85 degrees on the zRotate
Ring3 = 85 degrees on the zRotate
Pinky3 = 85 degrees on the zRotate

Now select the hand and set the xRotate to -90 degrees.

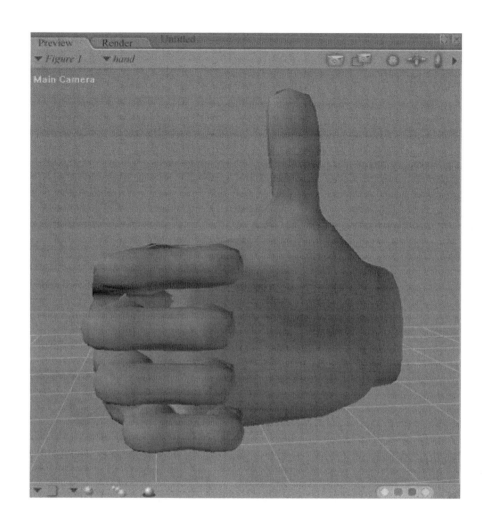

**THAT'S A BIG THUMBS UP. CONGRATULATIONS!**

## Chapter 6: Project 3
## Homeless Joe

This project will put together everything you've learned in Chapters 2 through 5. We'll be conducting this experiment on a guy I found living in the cardboard box next to mine behind the quickie mart. So don't worry if we kill him, nobody should notice him missing.

Oh wait, that's the other book I'm writing.

We'll still call him Homeless Joe but hopefully by the time we're done he'll be welcome in your runtime.

Let's go ahead and create a folder in the Poser runtime folder for Characters called MaleProj3. Then copy the MaleProj3.OBJ over to this folder.

## Part 1: UVMapper

I know, this seems boring. We always start with UVMapper. Well ... we have to. So start it up and stop complaining.

Load MaleProj3.OBJ into UVMapper. Your screen should look something like Figure 6-1.

Fig 6-1

Kind of looks like the Tiny Dancer when we first started out ... only worse!

So let's see about getting a little better look at this guy. Use the Edit > New UV Map > Planar to set it up. Be sure the Alignment is on Z-Axis and Don't Split is selected and click OK.

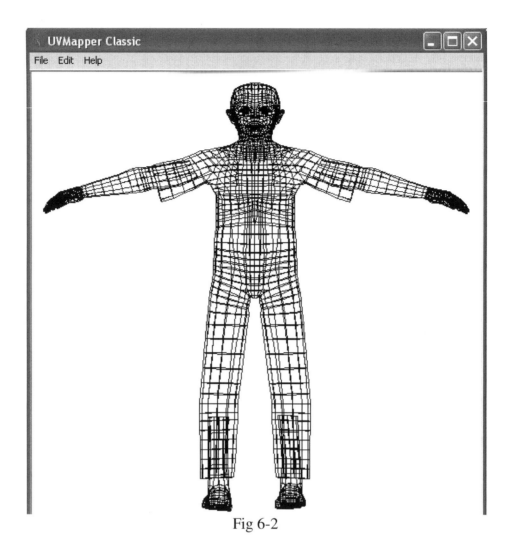
Fig 6-2

Now things look a little better in Figure 6-2. So let's look at how we are going to dismember this guy.

If you look at the basic breakdown as shown in Figure 6-3, you'll notice it is pretty much the same as it was for Tiny Dancer.

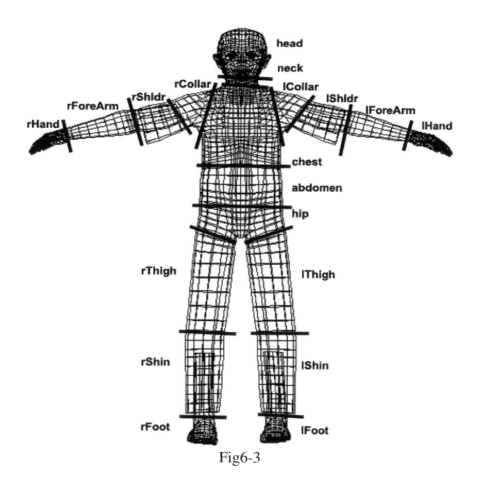

Fig6-3

But as you can see the mesh is much more complex and will require multiple cuts to name many of the groups. Also, on this character, we will be breaking down the hands to fully joint them and we will also be splitting the foot so that there are 'toes' so the foot can bend when the character walks. And we will make Homeless Joe walk.

So let's start cutting Joe up according to the diagram in Figure 6-3. As before, we will be starting with the hands and moving into the shldr cutting, naming and making the parts invisible on each side as we go. Then we'll be cutting and naming the legs up to the hip. As with Tiny Dancer, when we have chopped off all of Joe's arms and legs, drag a selection box over the top of him from corner to corner and enlarge him using the Edit > New UV Map > Planar command, making sure that the alignment is still on the Z-Axis and Don't Split is selected.

Your display should look something like Figure 6-4.

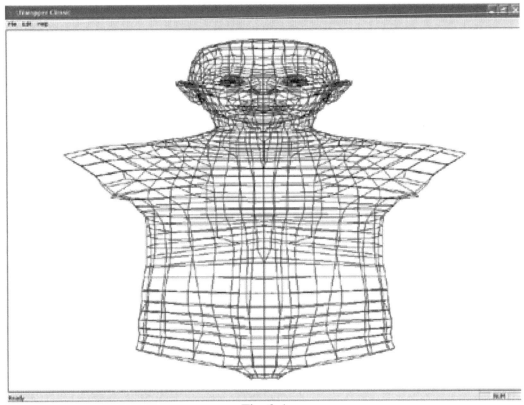

Fig 6-4

I heard some of you ask, why didn't we cut up the hands and feet? Well, that's a good question with a simple answer. To cut up the hands and feet you need to view them both from a different alignment, the Y-Axis. You also need to display them larger on the screen for greater accuracy. So for these two reasons it is best to save them for last and do them after all the major body parts have been named and hidden.

Now let's continue cutting up Joe before he crawls back to his box behind the quickie mart.

Go ahead and separate the hip and abdomen and then enlarge the remaining mesh for a better view at the chest and collars. Your display should now look like Figure 6-5.

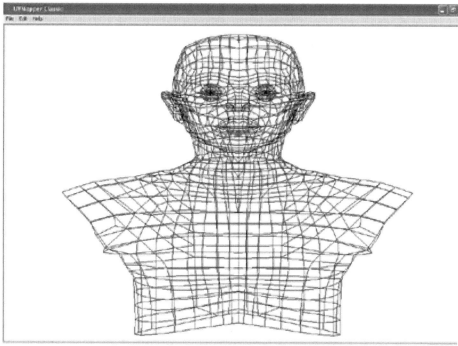
Fig 6-5

Now we can more easily separate the collars from the chest. Go ahead and make these groups and hide them. Your model should now look something like Figure 6-6.

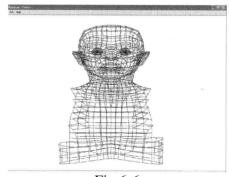
Fig 6-6

Now we can more easily separate the chest from the neck. This will take several cuts and moving of groups. But things should look something like Figure 6-7 when you are ready to name the chest parts.

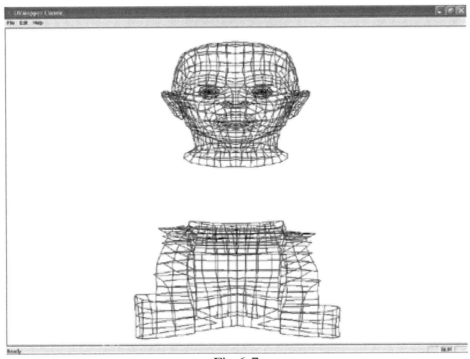

Fig 6-7

But before we name and hide the chest let's take a look at it from the side to see if we accidentally grabbed part of the neck too. Go ahead and drag a selection box around the parts of the chest and use the Edit > New UV Map > Planar command to change the view. Be sure to select X-Axis for alignment and Don't Split before clicking OK.

The view should look something like Figure 6-8.

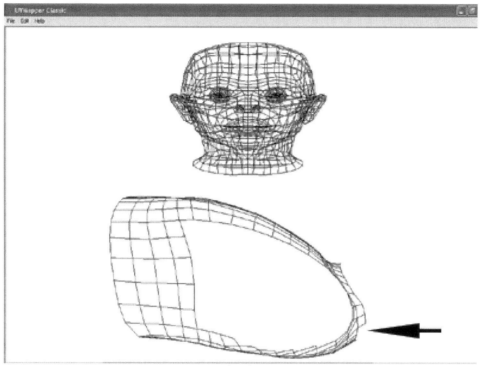
Fig 6-8

If you look at where the arrow is pointing you'll notice I missed a few polys on the back of the neck. You may have gotten them. But no matter, we can fix that when we view the neck and head from the side. So let's go ahead and select the chest, name it, and hide it.

Now draw a selection box over the head and neck so that it is larger than the head and neck and resize it and switch to the side view using the Edit > New UV Map > Planar command. Alignment and Split should still be on the X-Axis and Don't Split from switching the view on the chest, so click OK. Your screen should now look like Figure 6-9.

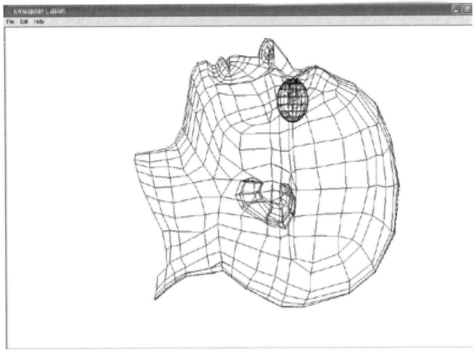

Fig 6-9

We can now easily see the polygons at the base of the neck that belong to the chest and can easily see where the neck and head join to separate them. First select the polys that belong to the chest and name them and hide them. Then go ahead and select the neck and name it and hide it. Finally, select the head and name it and hide it too.

Note: At this point we could separate out both of the eyes from the head mesh and name them so that they work, but that is a little beyond the scope of this book.

Now we are ready to start working in the hands. In the Edit Menu, click Select > by Group and highlight lHand from the list. Click OK. A selection box will be on the screen where the lHand is located. Click Ctrl+} to make the lHand visible and then resize it to fit the major portion of the screen as shown in Figure 6-10.

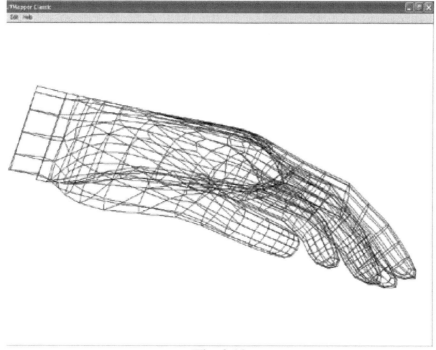

Fig 6-10

As you can probably see there are a few stray polys attached to the hand at the wrist that should probably be part of the lForeArm. Go ahead and select them and add them to the lForeArm and then make them invisible. Now select the entire hand and change the view so that we are looking at it on the Y-Axis. The display should now look like Figure 6-11 after you separate the joints of the fingers and thumb.

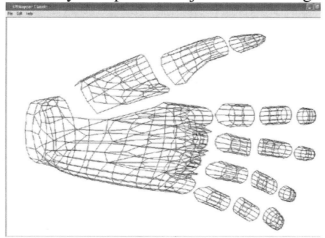

Fig 6-11

Even though this hand is sculpted differently from the one used in Project 2, the procedures described in Chapter 5 for creating the joints still applies. You may have to make multiple selections to create the groups as pictured so be patient and take your time grouping them and naming them according to the instruction in Chapter 5. Also, remember to place an l (that's a small letter L not a number 1) in front of each joint name so that it is identified for the left hand side.

When you have finished doing the left hand and all the parts for it are hidden, go ahead and do the same for the right hand being sure to place an r in front of each joint name to identify it as being for the right hand.

Now let's look at Joe's feet. Your screen should be blank at this time so using the Edit > Select > by Group command, highlight first the lFoot and then use the scroll bar to scan down to the rFoot. While holding down the Ctrl key click the rFoot. Both the left and right foot should now be highlighted in the menu so click OK to show the selection box around where they are located on the screen. Click Ctrl+} to make the feet visible. While the selection box is still active, grab one of the corner sizing handles and resize the feet so that they fill the screen a little better. When you have done that, use the Edit > New UV Map > Planar command to change the view to the Y-Axis and Don't Split. The display should now look something like Figure 6-12.

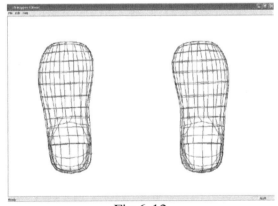

Fig 6-12

In case you haven't guessed by now, when you are looking at a mesh in Y-Axis in UV Mapper, you are looking at it from the bottom up. See in Figure 6-12 the foot on the left hand side of the screen is the rFoot, and the one on the right hand side of the screen is the lFoot.

Select the tips of each foot as shown in Figure 6-13 and name them rToe and lToe.

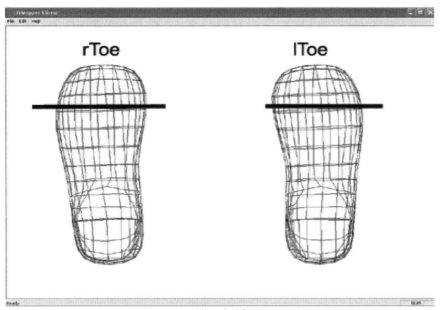

Fig 6-13

We are now done naming all the body parts for Joe, so go ahead and save the OBJ back to the MaleProj3 folder in the Poser Runtime Characters folder and name it HomelessJoe.OBJ.

We're done with UVMapper for now so go ahead and shut it down.

## Part 2: PHI-Builder

Now we are ready to jump back into PHI-Builder and set up the basic joints for Homeless Joe. Go ahead and start PHI-Builder and load the OBJ for Homeless Joe. You should be looking at a screen similar to the one in Figure 6-14.

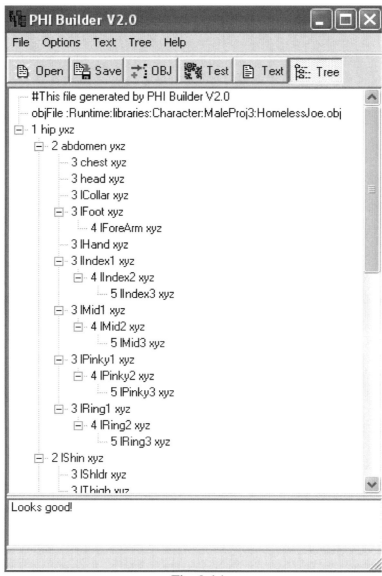

Fig 6-14

Wow, this one is HUGE. It doesn't even fit on the screen. And once again if a human body could be jointed this way we'd have something that would scare HP Lovecraft half silly.

So how do we attack something this huge? One piece at a time. If you look closely you'll see that all the left fingers are lined up under the left hand. So let's go ahead and drag them onto the left hand so that they are in the right place.

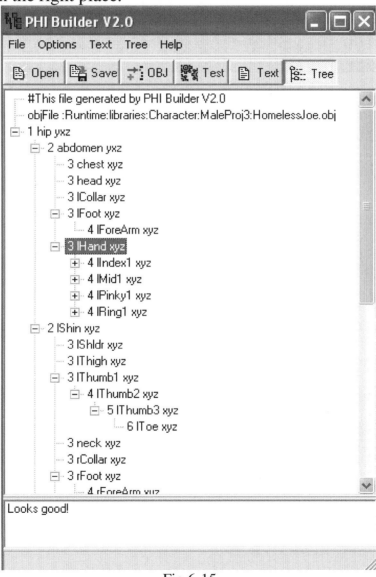

Fig 6-15

Ok, in Figure 6-15 we can see where the lThumb is but before we move it to the lHand we have to move the lToe off the lThumb to the lFoot. Go ahead and drag the toe to the foot and then the thumb to the hand. Things should look something like Figure 6-16.

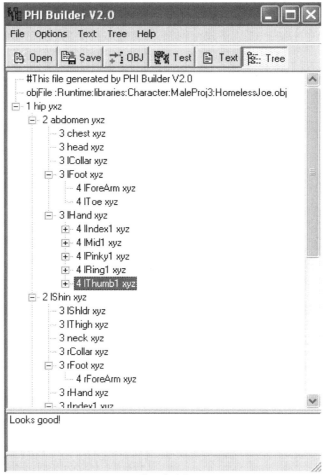

Fig 6-16

Since the hierarchy collapses as we drag a joint to it's higher companion, let's go ahead and drag some pretty quickly as follows:

lHand onto the lForeArm
lForeArm onto the lShldr
lShldr onto the lCollar
and finally
lCollar onto the chest

With those moved to their proper places, the screen should look something like Figure 6-17

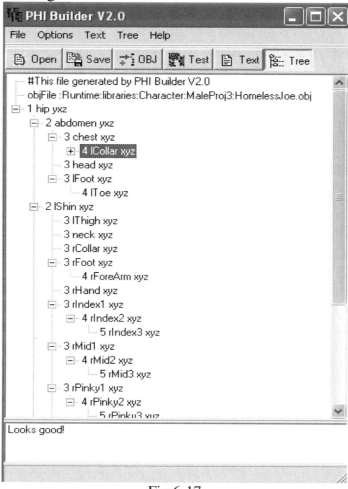

Fig 6-17

Now the left arm is completely collapsed and the rest of the hierarchy is becoming visible to work on. You can now see where the right fingers are in relation to the right hand. So go ahead and drag the fingers onto the hand; and then the hand onto the forearm; and the forearm onto the shldr; and then the shldr onto the collar; and finally attach the collar to the chest as we did with the left arm.

At this point the hierarchy should look like Figure 6-18.

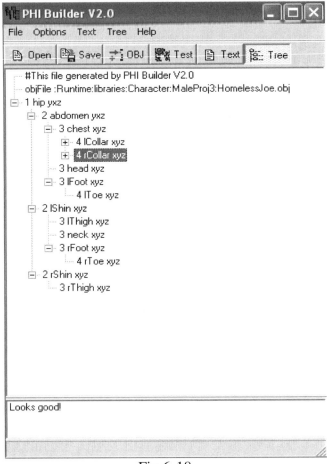

Fig 6-18

Did you remember to move the rToe from the rThumb before attaching the thumb to the hand? If not, expand the right arm hierarchy by clicking the +'s until you find the rToe and drag it over to the rFoot.

OK, now let's drag the rThigh to the hip, followed by the rShin to the rThigh, and then drag the rFoot to the rShin.

Now drag the neck off of the lShin and attach it to the chest. Then attach the head to the neck.

Finally, drag the lThigh to the hip, the shin to the thigh and the foot to the shin.

Your screen should now look something like Figure 6-19.

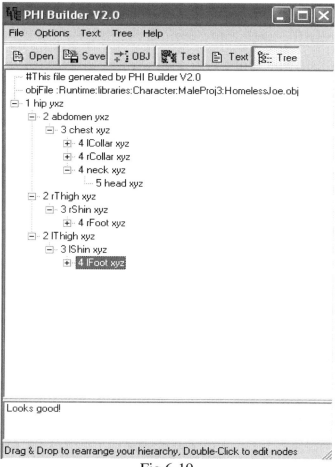

Fig 6-19

The hierarchy should now be properly arranged and ready for us to look at the rotation orders of the joints.

As explained earlier, all joints that Twist on the vertical axis (Y-Axis) should have a rotation order of YZX. This would include the following joints: abdomen, chest, neck, head, both thighs, both shins, and both feet. If you look at Figure 6-19 only the abdomen is even close. Go ahead and fix these joints by double clicking them to open the dialog box with the rotation orders. Highlight the dot by the YZX rotation for each of these joints and click OK.

If the plus sign is still active on both feet after setting the rotations, go ahead and click it to look at the rotation order of the toes. As discussed earlier in the book, the Twist rotation for the Toes is on the Z-Axis and should be ZYX. Go ahead and change these and now we'll take a look at the arms.

The hierarchy for the arms is probably still collapsed from when we reordered the structure. So go ahead and click the plus sign in front of the lCollar to expand the hierarchy. Continue clicking the +'s as the joints expand until all the joints for the left arm are exposed as shown in Figure 6-20

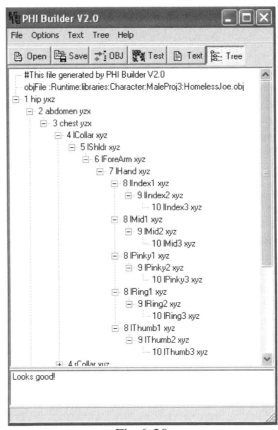

Fig 6-20

The X Twist for all of these joints is acceptable for all but one of the joints and we'll get to that one in just a minute. First let's look at the last two rotations of Y and Z. These are also fine for everything except the ForeArm as discussed in Chapter 4 for the Tiny Dancer. This joint should Bend on the Y Axis. So change this joint rotation to XZY.

Now let's look at the thumb. As you hopefully remember from Chapter 5, when we set the thumb rotation we used the order of ZYX. This hand is modeled in a more natural pose from the one used in that chapter and Twist seems to run through the finger on the X rotation. While we could use that for all of the joints in the thumb, a potentially better rotation for the first joint of the thumb is probably the ZYX rotation we used on the other hand. The reason for this is because this joint will rotate for the most part on the X and Y Axis for moving Up and Down and Clasping into a fist. The Z rotation will probably not be used at all. So for the first joint of the thumb, set the rotation order at ZYX. This probably seems contrary to what was said before about rotation orders but there is an exception to every rule and the first thumb joint is sometimes that exception.

Now go ahead and set the joints we discussed above for the left the same way for the right arm.

Are we done with PHI-Builder now?

Who said yes? You've failed the course. Pack up your things and get out of here.

Who said we still need to set IK? Give that person a gold star.

Yes, in PHI-Builder we still need to set the IK. But this time we are not only going to set it for the legs, we are also going to set it for the arms. For some reason when a Poser character has hands with working fingers, Poser seems to forget that the hand is attached at the wrist to the forearm. When you apply a pose to a character without IK on the Arms, the hands tend to go flying off into space and the forearm gets all twisted out of shape.

Do you remember how to set IK? First make sure you have the hip selected and click on the Tree in the menu above the icon menu. Then from that drop down select Add IK Chain... In the text space for the IK Chain name type LeftLeg (or RightLeg, LeftArm, RightArm) select the first node (lThigh for the LeftLeg or one of the collars for the right or left arm) and then select the last node (lFoot for the LeftLeg or one of the hands for the arms). Now click OK. Do this for

Fig 6-21

each leg and each arm. Your screen should look like Figure 6-21 when finished.

Now we are finished with PHI-Builder. Click save and type HomelessJoe for the file name and save it to the MaleProj3 folder.

Almost there ...

## Part 3: Poser

Now we can load Homeless Joe into Poser and hopefully find a home for him.

Click File > Convert Hier... and navigate to where you left HomelessJoe.PHI sleeping on the street corner. Give him a good swift kick in the PHI file and when you get the text box asking for his name, type: HomelessJoe.

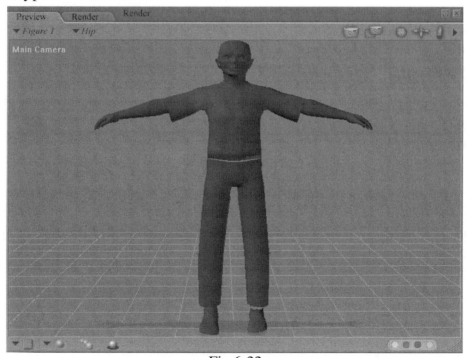

Fig 6-22

Now wander over to the New Figures folder and load Joe so we can look at him. He should look something like Figure 6-22.

We may have some reversed normals right now, but we're not going to worry about them. Let's get Joe walking.

In the Poser menu, click Window > Walk Designer to load the Walk Designer portion of the program. Accept all the defaults and click Apply. In the window that is displayed, click the Radio Button for Walk in Place and close the window. Now exit the Walk Designer and click play to watch Joe walk to his new home.

Joe thanks you, and I thank you, for helping him get on his feet so that he could get a better life.

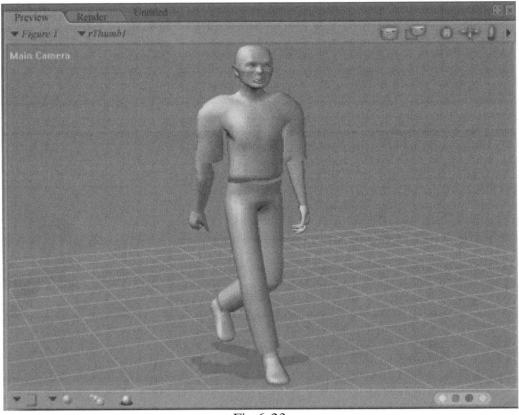
Fig 6-23

## Chapter 7: Dr. Strange Bend
or
## How I learned to stop worrying and love the Joint Editor.

No apologies to Stanley, sorry!

Yes, we are going to delve into the bane of the Poser user, the dreaded Joint Editor. The place where normal peoples knuckles become white, they gnash their teeth together until their gums bleed, and then they go running off screaming in search of the first train they can find to throw themselves under it.

Well, maybe not that bad, but pretty close.

Figure 7-1 shows a good, basic screen setup for a single monitor system when setting JPs.

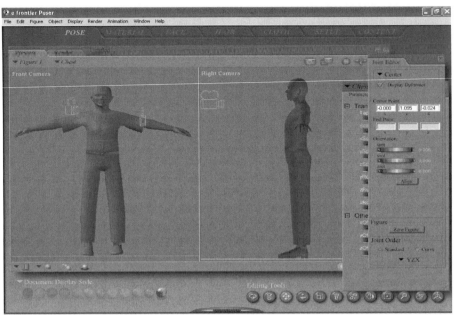

Fig 7-1

I usually keep one view panel on the front camera and switch the second view between right, left, and top camera depending on what joint I am working on and what kind of view I need to see. I also use the Zoom Tool in the Editing Tool bar to zoom in on joints that I am working on for fine tuning.

But first let's look at the Joint Editor itself.

I see you in the back sneaking out to find a train ... sit back down and listen! It's not that hard. At least not as hard as it looks.

Figure 7-2 shows the basic panel for the joint editor and the drop down for what items of a joint that can be edited. On the left hand side you can ignore pretty much everything below the boxes for the center x,y,z location. On the right hand side in the drop down menu you can ignore pretty much everything below the last Rotate item. We will look at the Orientation dials a little bit, but don't worry, they're easy too once you understand them.

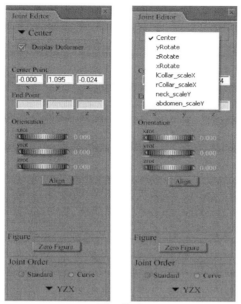

Fig 7-2

Although you can work the joints in any order you want, I usually work top to bottom. Left side to right side. So let's select the head and start there.

With the head selected zoom in both view panels until your screen is similar to Figure 7-3.

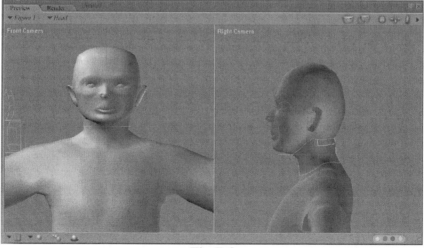

Fig 7-3

Of course you'll probably have the Joint Editor up on the screen somewhere but I'm cropping the image to make the illustration more clear.

With the Joint Editor active you will note the red cross hair at the top of the head and the green cross hair at the base of the head. These are the center of the joint rotation. The red cross shows the end limit of the joint rotation while the green one is the actual rotation point.

Looking at things from the front, the green cross looks OK. But looking at it from the right you can see that it is way to far forward and probably a little low for where the spine would connect to the skull. To move the cross, make sure you have the right camera selected and put the cursor over the center of the green cross hair. The cursor will turn into a bullseye meaning you are lined up on it. Left click on the mouse to grab the crosshair and drag it back about two-thirds of the width of the neck and move it up to the base of the skull as shown in Figure 7-4.

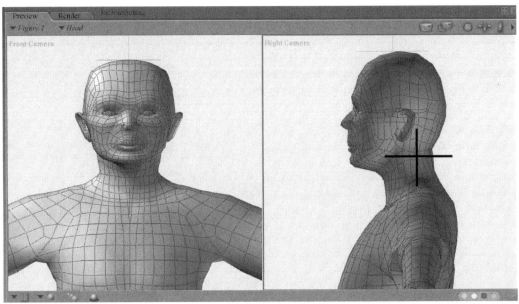

Fig 7-4

I've highlighted the location of the green cross so that you can see it better in Figure 7-4. This is a much better location for the head to join the neck. But we still need to look at the rotations and the limits for this joint.

Let's do the Twist. No, not the dance, the joint rotation for the head. From the drop down box in the Joint Editor, select the yRotate from the menu. As you better remember, the head Twists on the Y-Axis. Now look at Figure 7-5 on the Right Camera view to see where the Y-Axis runs through the head.

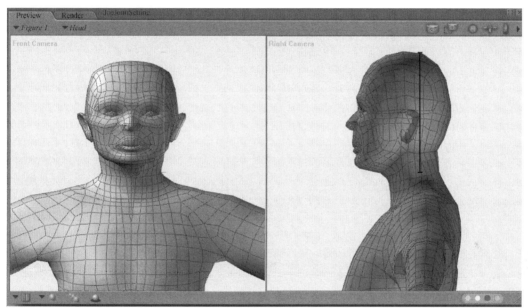

Fig 7-5

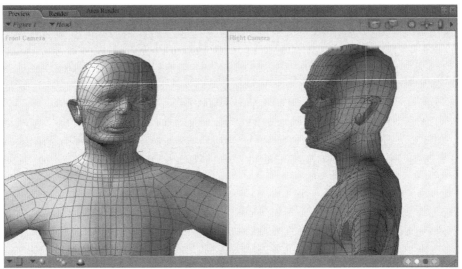

Fig 7-6

I've darkened the line so you can more easily see it in the illustration. Now using the pose dials on the head, turn the head about 40 degrees on the yRotate. See how it distorts in Figure 7-6?

Now grab the red handle at the bottom of the vertical line that represents the Y-Axis and when you have the Bullseye, click and drag down until the handle lines up with the top of the shoulder. You

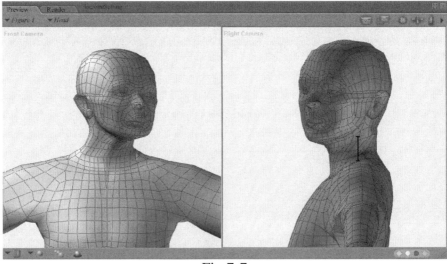

Fig 7-7

should see the back of the neck adjust to a more natural curve. Then grab the green handle at the top of the vertical line and drag down and watch the face slowly correct itself. When you reach the level of the chin, the head should look something like Figure 7-7.

Congratulations, you've just set your first joint rotation. And in answer to the question in your head, YES, setting most of the joints is that easy and can be done visually. Go ahead and set the yRotate dial for the head back to zero.

Now let's move onto the next rotation for the head in the drop down list of the Joint Editor. The next one should be the zRotate. Since this one is the side to side motion of the head, we need to work on this one using the Front Camera. Go ahead and select that camera and look at how the joint describer changes from the straight line to two 90 degree angles, one green and one red, that angle away from each at the center. These are called the include and exclude angles as shown

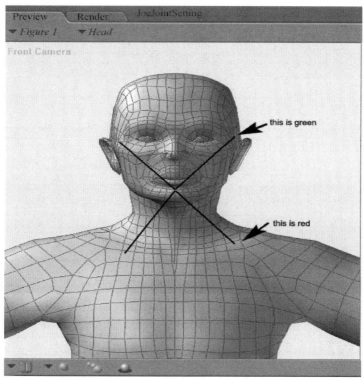

Fig 7-8

in Figure 7-8.

Now using the zRotate dial twist the head to the right or the left about 30 degrees. See how the head and area where the neck meets the shoulder distorts in Figure 7-9?

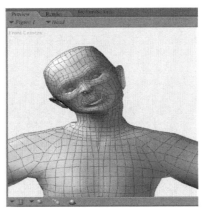
Fig 7-9

If we adjust the include and exclude angles to a position similar to

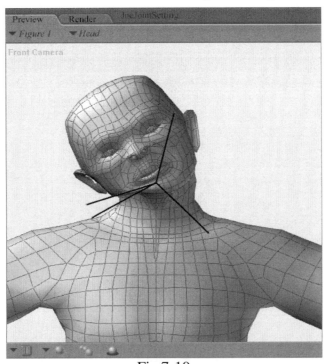
Fig 7-10

what is shown in Figure 7-10 you will notice that the neck/shoulder area cleans up pretty good, but the face is still distorted around the chin. This is actually acceptable since when we set the limits for this joint, the head will not be able to tilt anymore than 8 to 10 degrees to the right or to the left. Most side to side bending is done in the neck.

Now reset the zRotate back to zero and set the angles of the other side of the include/exclude similar to the left side. Then in the Joint Editor select xRotate from the drop down list. On the xRotate dial for the head, set the dial at about -60 degrees. Your display should look something like a snooty English butler as pictured in Figure 7-11.

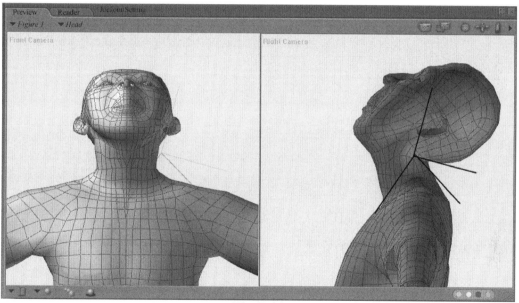

Fig 7-11

To make it so he doesn't drown when it rains, grab the end of the green angle pointing almost straight up and drag it down so that it is under the chin. The head should look more like Figure 7-12 now.

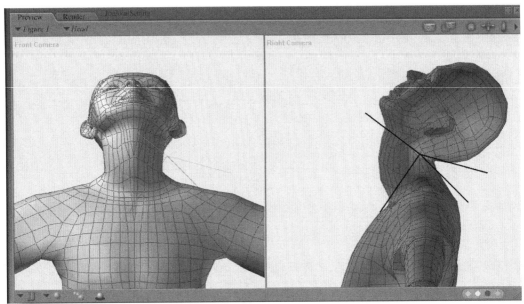

Fig 7-12

All the joint rotations for the head are now set and there was no need to go looking for that train.

It's a good idea now to play with the head a little moving it on all the different rotations to make sure it looks OK. If you want you can fine tune some of the settings and maybe see what other setting might do. But for now these settings are fine for this character and we can move on to the neck.

Using the same methods described above, go ahead and set the center and rotations for the neck based on the image sequence below in Figure 7-13.

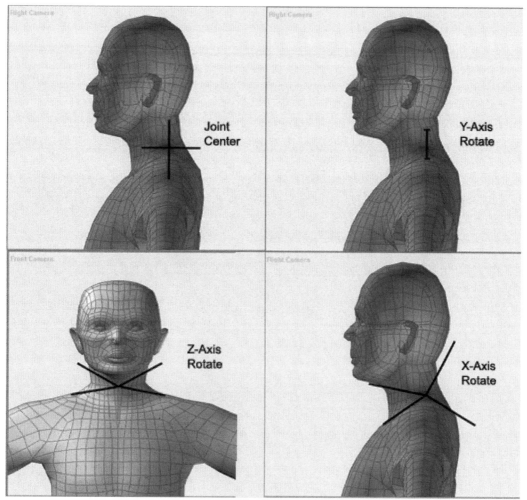

Fig 7-13

By now you should be starting to see how the joint settings work. In these situations, everything above the green mark or angle is what moves freely with the joint (include). Everything below the red mark or angle is what remains stationary (exclude). All the parts in between the two marks or angles is what is used to blend the bending of the joint together. Voila' ... include angle, exclude angle, blend zone.

"So what are the spherical falloff zones?", you may ask. They are a way to refine a joint that cannot be totally defined with the three basic parameters. They are optional and can be left turned off for most joints. But when there are areas where three or more body parts are closely grouped together, the spherical falloffs help to isolate one joint away from another to avoid interference between them.

Using what you have learned above, go ahead and set the joints for the chest and abdomen using the reference images in Figure 7-14 adjusting your screen views as needed to see the body parts you are working on.

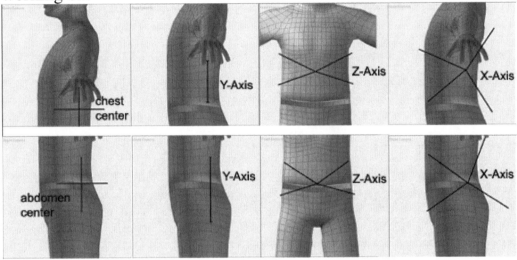
Fig 7-14

Some of you are probably wondering why I'm not giving an anatomy lesson to explain how to set joints. The reason is because I'm NOT giving an anatomy lesson. I'm showing you how to set joints in Poser. While 75% to 80% of the anatomy rules apply in Poser, the other 20% to 25% is guess work and just 'getting it to look right'. Which sometimes you just won't be able to do and you'll just have to live with a bad joint. When setting joints you can think in terms of soft tissue and hard tissue and it will help as you look at how YOUR body moves and bends and how you can relate that to how you want your Poser character to move and bend. Such as the stomach area. You want a large blending area in the front as opposed to less blending in the rear. Why? The spine is a hard tissue area as opposed to the soft tissues of the stomach. The images above may appear to have the same amount of blend on the X-Axis, but consider where the joint is located in the middle of the spine. This gives you a much larger blend area in the stomach as compared to the area of the spine that is blended.

Dammit Jim, I'm a Poser Rigger, not a doctor! Enough anatomy, let's move on to the legs.

So let's look at the left leg. The left thigh inparticular where it joins the hip. We always need to look at the center of the joint first to make sure the joint is aligned properly. Look at Figure 7-15 for centering the lThigh joint.

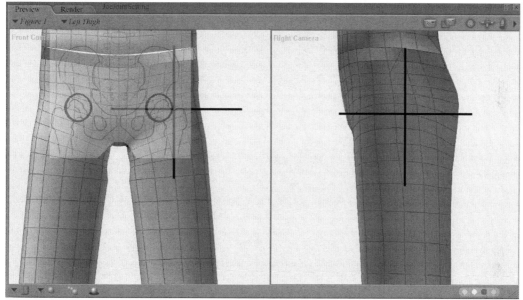

Fig 7-15

For you people who wanted an anatomy lesson, you'll like Figure 7-15. From the Right Camera view the joint is centered fine. But from the Front Camera view with the human hip bone configuration superimposed over Joe, we can see that the center should be moved to about the center of the circle indicating the socket for the thigh. Visually go ahead and move the center point over to this location and now look at the Orientation dials. The thigh bone doesn't line up vertically like the spine does so we have to adjust that orientation to match the leg. If you turn the zrot dial to about 8 degrees you will see the Y-Axis line shift to match the angle of the leg as shown in Figure 7-16.

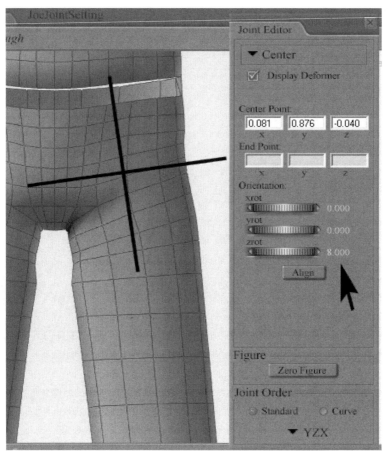

Fig 7-16

This will allow the thigh to Twist on the Y-Axis more naturally and move on the other axis' in a smoother way.

Now from the drop down select yRotate so we can set the Twist of the leg. Using the yRotate dial on the lThigh, twist the leg back and forth and watch how the hip deforms. You will notice the leg works pretty good, but there are problems with the way the hip deforms on the right side as shown by the marks in Figure 7-17.

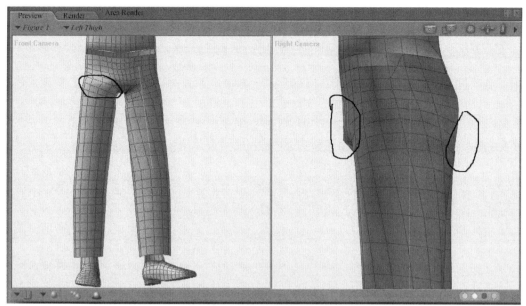

Fig 7-17

Although you could fix this by dropping down the red handle of the Y-Axis until the deformations were gone, this would also remove the deformations on the left side of the hip that we do want. This is one of the joints where the spherical falloff zones come into play. Reset the yRotate of the lThigh back to zero and then click the box marked Spherical Falloff Zones in the Joint Editor to turn them on. Two

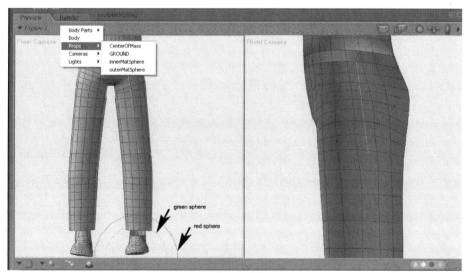

Fig 7-18

circles, a green one and a red one, will appear at the bottom of the display over the left foot as shown in Figure 7-18.

In the drop down menu for Props, as shown in Figure 7-18, these are identified as the innerMatSphere and outerMatSphere. You may ask why they are listed here and not in the Joint Editor menu. The answer? Who knows. It's just one of the more oddball things about Poser. Obviously the innerMatSphere is the green circle and the outer is the red. Go ahead and click on the outerMatSphere in the Props menu and we'll work on getting it positioned first.

Selecting the outerMatSphere will make it the selected item in the Properties control. All of the normal controls for moving and sizing the sphere are there. A good starting point for the outerMatSphere is as shown in Figure 7-19.

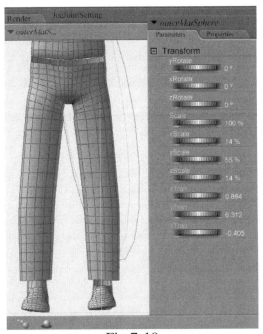

Fig 7-19

The settings used are as follows:

| | |
|---|---|
| xScale | 14.00% |
| yScale | 55.00% |
| zScale | 14.00% |
| xTrans | 0.85 |
| yTrans | 6.31 |
| zTrans | -0.41 |

These settings can also be used as a starting point for setting the innerMatSphere location. Select it from the Props menu and enter these settings. Twist the thigh to the right or the left to get an idea of what the distortion is and then play with the settings of the innerMatSphere until you have something that looks like Figure 7-20.

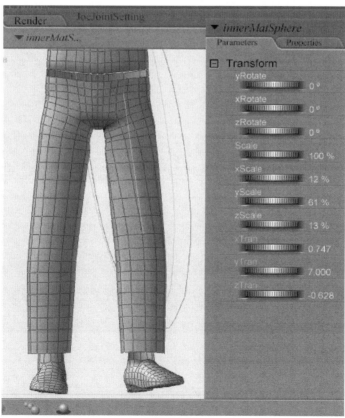

Fig 7-20

As you adjust the position and size of the innerMatSphere, the leg geometry will correct and you can visually see when it looks right. The settings used above are pretty good but some fine tuning could be done between the red and green spheres to better tune the falloff zones. Feel free to play with this and see what you can come up with. But at least now, the twisting of the thigh doesn't cause the right leg to deform with the left leg. All deformation is in the groin and up the left side of the hip where is should be.

Now we'll set the zRotate. Select it from the drop down on the Joint Editor and make sure the Front Camera is selected and the lThigh is the active body part. Adjust the zRotate angle for the lThigh to about 25 degrees. The joint distortion in the groin area will look similar to the the left hand side of Figure 7-21.

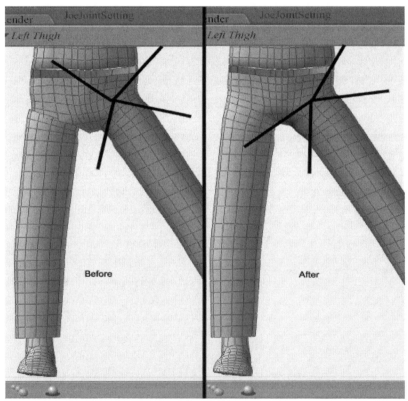

Fig 7-21

Adjust the red and green angles to similar positions as shown in the right hand side of the image and watch the joint correct itself. Since the include/exclude angles naturally isolate this joint from the right leg, there is really no point in setting spherical falloff zones. Reset the angle of the leg back to zero and let's move on to the xRotate.

In the drop down box of the Joint Editor select xRotate. On the Properties panel for the lThigh, rotate the thigh on the x-Axis about -75 degrees. If you look at Figure 7-22 you'll notice that the rotation point does a pretty good job when looked at it from the Right Camera.

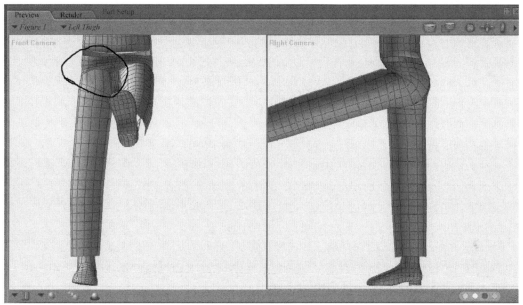
Fig 7-22

But the Front Camera, as indicated by the rough circle, shows that the entire front of the hip collapses and part of the rThigh is deformed. This joint needs Spherical Falloff Zones real bad to make it look right.

Before we set the Spherical Zones, let's tighten up the include/exclude just a bit to define the crease where the front of the thigh hits the hip as shown in Figure 7-23.

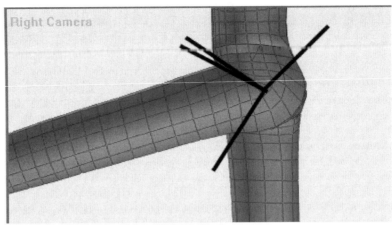

Fig 7-23

Now reset the xRotate back to zero and turn on the Spherical Falloff Zones in the Joint Editor. You should now have a red and green circle around the left foot same as when we turned on the SFZs for the yRotate.

From the Props menu select the OuterMatSphere and on it's Properties list enter the same information you used for the Y-Axis OuterMatSphere. Now select the InnerMatSphere and on it's Properties list enter the same settings you had for the Y-Axis InnerMatsphere. Look at the lThigh rotated at -75 degrees again as

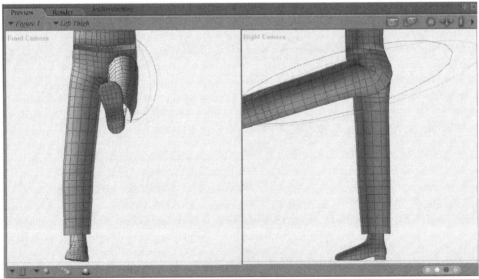

Fig 7-24

shown in Figure 7-24.

As you can see, the same setting works for both the Y and X Axis. The xRotate could be refined a little just as the other could, but these setting work well enough to show you what can be done and how easy it actually is to do it.

Reset the xRotate to zero on the lThigh Properties and let's move on to the lShin.

With the lShin selected, test the leg movement using the yRotate. Hmm, looks pretty good. Now test the zRotate. That's looks pretty good too. Now let's try the xRotate. Wow, that looks pretty good too. We're done, let's move on to the lFoot.

The lesson learned above? If it ain't broke, don't fix it!

Let's try the same thing with the lFoot now. Oops, yRotate doesn't look too good. The zRotate doesn't look bad but the x does. Oh well, it was worth a try. But let's look at why the foot didn't work like the shin. In the Joint Editor select Center from the drop down box and look at the Right Camera view as shown in Figure 7-25.

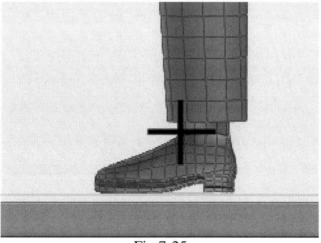

Fig 7-25

As you can see the rotation center is too far forward for the Y and X Axis to work properly but would allow the Z to work fine. So drop the cursor over the cross in the Right Camera view and when you have the bullseye drag it to the center of the ankle. This will correct the blending of the foot to shin a lot, but a little adjustment to the include/exclude angles will help. Look at the settings as shown in Figure 7-26 to get an idea of what the angles should be so that the bottom of the pants and the top of the foot stop distorting.

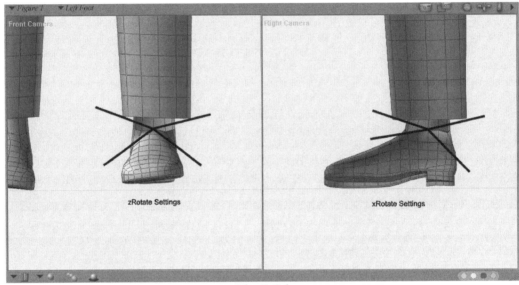

Fig 7-26

OK, let's move on to the lToe and see how it performs. This one is an oddball, remember, that twists on the Z-Axis. So let's check that first ... hmmm looks pretty good. Go ahead and check the yRotate which would be the side to side motion. Ditto. How about the xRotate. We have a winner. No need to set any of the angles here, they work fine.

Now let's shift the camera view north to line up on the collar/shoulder area on the left side as shown in Figure 7-27.

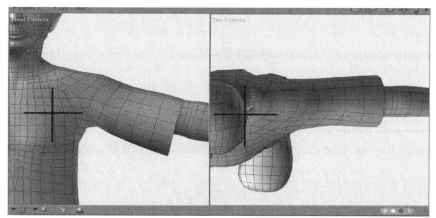

Fig7-27

You'll note that I have switched the Right Camera view for the Top Camera view and have moved it to better show the left shoulder area from above. This is needed to better view the way the joints work and how well we can get them to blend. Also note that I have gone ahead and highlighted the location of the center of the lCollar joint. As you can see, the center of the collar joint is probably too low as viewed from the front and needs to be moved back a little as viewed from the top. Go ahead and adjust these positions by dragging the center point with the bullseye cursor. A better position is shown in Figure 7-28

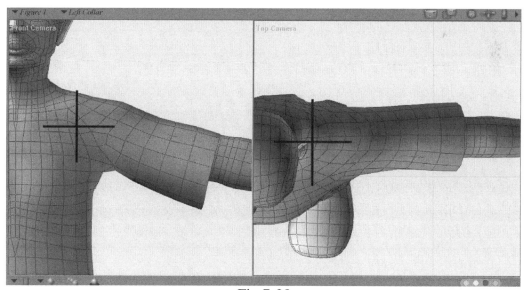

Fig 7-28

While this isn't a whole lot different from the original position, it will make for a better rotation center. But let's look at how the arm moves at this point on the xyz Axis'. Take a look at the image sequence in Figure 7-29.

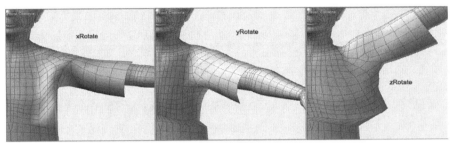

Fig 7-29

The center seems to be working pretty good but overall there is way too much of the chest being affected by the movement of the collar. Although some of this can be corrected using the include/exclude angles. Most of the problems for the xRotate and yRotate will have to be fixed with the spherical blend zones.

Let's start with the xRotate. Make sure all rotations are reset to zero, select xRotate from the drop down box on the Joint Editor, and then

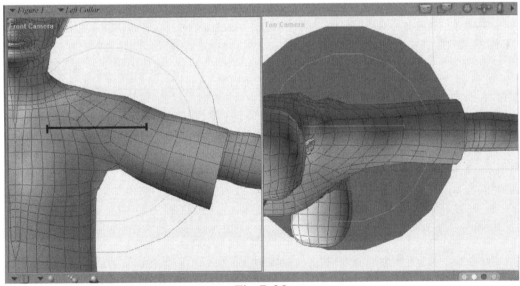

Fig 7-30

click Spherical Falloff Zones. From the Top Camera view you can see the red and green circles at Joe's feet. Go ahead and select the outer (red) circle from the Props menu and using the xyz Trans dials move it so that it is centered on the lCollar joint. Then do the same for the inner (green) circle. Your display should look something like Figure 7-30.

Please note that after moving the spherical zones into place, I enlarge the size of the xRotate line so that it encompasses more of the shoulder and chest. Play with the joint again and you will see that it is already starting to look better. So let's refine it a little now by adjusting the yScale of the spheres. A good starting point for the yScale of both spheres is around 10% as shown in Figure 7-31.

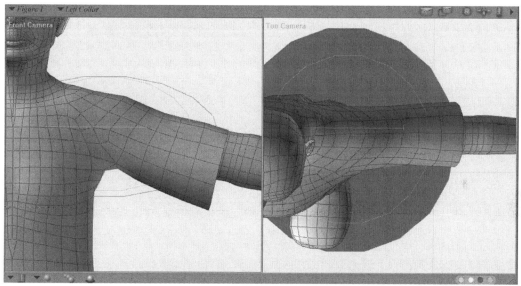
Fig 7-31

Play with the joint again on the xRotate and see how much better it blends now. Yes, on extremes it still distorts, but you have to remember that the lCollar and the lShldr joints work together to make the arm blend into the upper chest properly. What we can't get in terms of movement with the collar, will be completed with the shoulder. So let's move on to the yRotate.

In the Joint Editor select the yRotate from the drop down box and click Spherical Falloff Zones to activate them. Again you can see the red and green circles in the Top Camera view. Select each circle and using the Properties dials adjust the xyz Trans so that the circles are centered on the collar joint same as for the xRotate. In fact you can probably use the same settings to start with. Now play with the include/exclude angles and the size and locations of the SFZs. You may or may not come up with something similar to Figure 7-32, but what you come up with may work better. Figure 7-32 is a good starting point though.

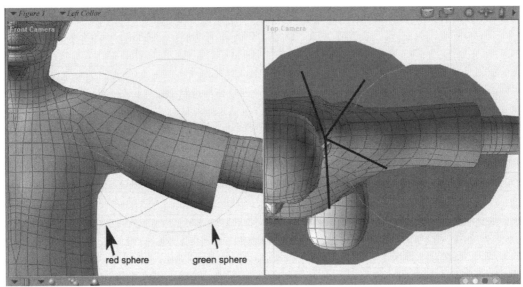

Fig 7-32

As you can see, the spheres don't have to be one inside the other. They can overlap allowing for better defining of what is and is not affected in the blending. Also note that only the outer sphere has been reshaped a little on the Y-Axis to control how much blending there is under the arm. The inner sphere is moved out along the length of the arm so that the blending between the collar/shoulder into the chest area is greater while the affect on the upper arm is reduced. Also notice how the exclude angles have been moved to reduce the affect of the bend on the chest to include only the left most part of the chest and back. This is not a perfect joint, but it is a good place to start playing with the joint to improve it.

Let's look at zRotate.

The zRotate is another joint that can be set visually. Set the zRotate of the collar so that the arm is pointing at an extreme angle up. Using the bullseye cursor select the ends of the exclude angle and move them around until you've excluded most of the chest on the lower part of the angle and all of the neck on the upper part of the angle. For the include angle, move the ends around with the bullseye so that all of the upper and lower collar mesh is include and a good portion of the shoulder. At zero rotation the include and exclude angles should look something like Figure 7-33.

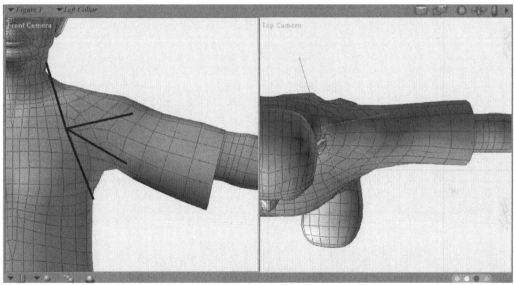

Fig 7-33

HEY MOM, LOOK, NO SFZs AGAIN!

With Spherical Falloff Zones the basic rule is if you don't really need to set them: Don't. You CAN set them for EVERY joint, and many content designers do (even I set them for a lot more than what I'm showing here most of the time), but this is a beginners guide and as such I'm showing you the basics of what you need to do to get by.

The collar is now done, let's move onto the lShldr.

Looking at the shoulder joint with the center selected in the Joint Editor you can see that the cross is fairly well centered in the Top Camera view but appears to be too low in the Front Camera view. Use the bullseye cursor to drag the cross up to a more centered position on the shoulder in the Front Camera view. Now you will notice that the X-Axis (Twist rotation) is pointing out of the arm instead of through

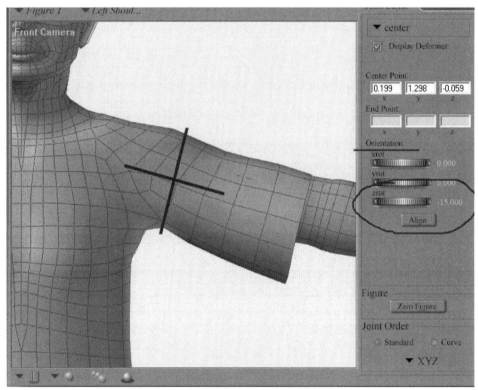

Fig 7-34

the arm. This is another joint, like the thigh, that will need to have the orientation fixed as shown in Figure 7-34.

A setting of -15 degrees appears to work well. Note: You could also click the Align button at the bottom of the Orientation box and it would give you a best guess for the orientation of the center. In many instances this is fine, but with the odd geometry of the body part (because of the shirt sleeve) the Align button would give a false setting. In many instances, it is best to adjust this visually by rotating the dials yourself.

With the orientation set, select xRotate from the drop down box of the Joint Editor. Twist the joint on the xRotate to see how it works. If you have the center or the joint approximately at the same location as shown in Figure 7-34, and have applied the orientation of -15 degrees, the twisting of the arm should look pretty good. So let's move on to the yRotate and give it a test.

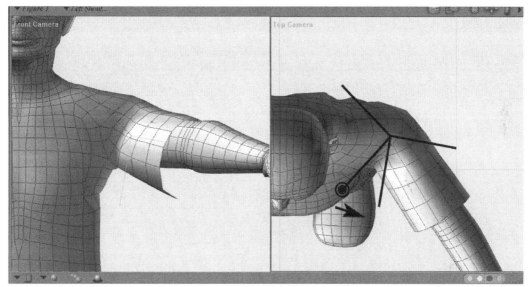
Fig 7-35

As you can see in the Front Camera view of Figure 7-35, there is a distortion under the arm in the side of the chest when the arm rotates forward. Using the Top Camera view as a guide, grab the front end of the exclude angle (red) with the bullseye cursor and drag it in the direction indicated towards the include (green) angle leg. The distortion will slowly disappear. When you try the yRotation now you will see that it works both front and back to a much better degree.

Now let's look at the zRotate. If you set the lShldr at -45 degrees on zRotate you will note that the underarm area collapses into the body as shown in Figure 7-36.

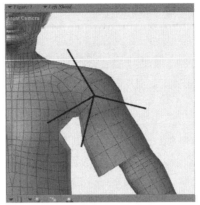
Fig 7-36

Obviously this is not acceptable but it looks like it might be able to be fixed by adjusting the lower leg of the exclude (red) angle. Go ahead and grab it with the bullseye and drag it towards the lower include (green) angle leg. You should end up with a blend like in Figure 7-37.

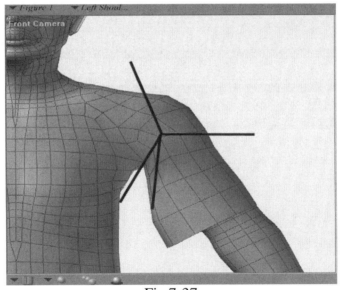
Fig 7-37

Note that I also adjusted the angle of the lower leg of the include (green) angle just a little to include more of the sleeve to give it a bit more of a natural hang.

To get a really good look for the blending of the shoulder area it is a good idea to play with combinations of the collar and shoulder bends to see what kind of fine tuning of the joints can be done to achieve the most natural look. That's your homework assignment. Let's move on to the lForeArm.

With Center selected from the drop down box in the Joint Editor, we can again see that the center of the joint is pretty well aligned in the Top Camera view but again it is a little low in the Front Camera view as shown in Figure 7-38.

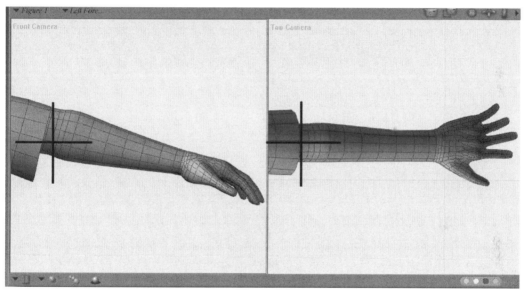
Fig 7-38

Using the bullseye cursor, go ahead and move the cross in the Front Camera view up so that it is more aligned to the center of the arm and the joint where the shoulder and forearm meet. After doing this, click the Align button in the Orientation box on the Joint Editor and see what happens. You should have something similar to Figure 7-39.

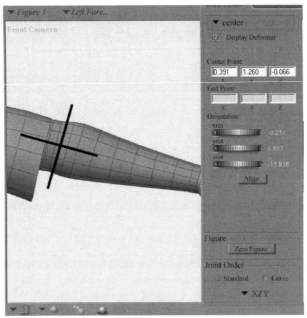

Fig 7-39

This orientation looks pretty good for the joint so let's see how well the joint works.

The xRotate looks pretty good. The zRotate doesn't really matter unless you plan on breaking the guy's arm. And finally the yRotate works pretty good too. Although the yRotate could be refined to include less of the bottom of the sleeve, it's fine for our purposes for now. We can always go back and do additional work on it later.

The lHand.

Because of it's odd shape, the hand joint center is off just a bit in both the Top and Right Camera views. Use the bullseye cursor to move the cross to the center of the joint in both views.

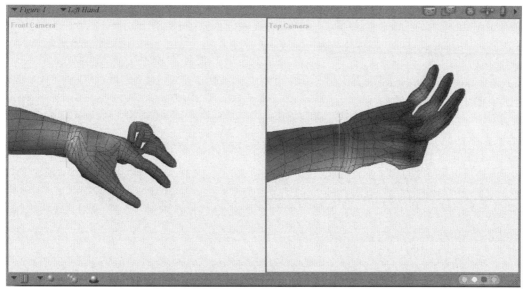

Fig 7-40

But when you test the hand you may be surprised to find there is something seriously wrong with this joint as shown in Figure 7-40. Don't panic. The joint has been reversed on the Y-Axis. What needs to be done is in the orientation box of the Joint Editor we need to set the yRotate at 180 degrees and the zRotate at -12.5 degrees as shown in Figure 7-41. (Note: Joint reversal may or may not happen.)

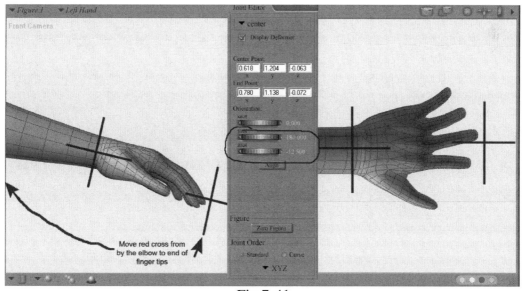

Fig 7-41

This will correct the wild distortions seen in Figure 7-40 but we still need to set the individual rotations ... or do we? Let's look at the xRotate now that we have the joint pointing in the right direction. As you can see the distortion is still pretty bad but can be fixed by dragging the include/exclude handles to the position shown in Figure 7-42

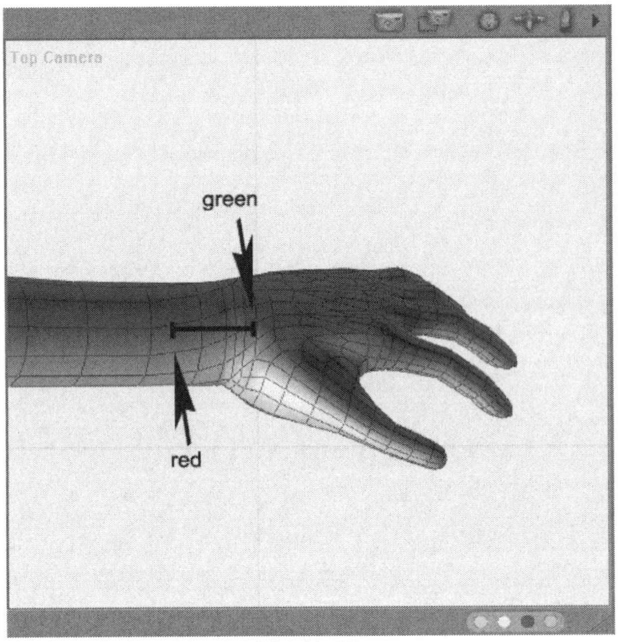

Fig 7-42

This will sound strange, but when you get the bullseye cursor, drag in the opposite direction of what you want the handle to go. For example, for the green end drag to the right to get it to go to the left. When you have the ends approximately where indicated in Figure 7-42, test the joint again in the xRotate to confirm it is working properly. (Note: This is because of the joint reversal above and may not occur if the joint does not reverse.)

Now the yRotate. Well, the yRotate actually works pretty good, as does the zRotate. So we can leave these alone and move on to the thumb.

The thumb can be a real bugger when it comes to setting up the joints.

Especially the first joint which depends greatly on how the hand was modeled. When we rigged Joe, we gave the first joint of the thumb a zyx rotation. Let's see how well that works now. As you play with the different rotations you will notice that basically they work pretty good even though the deformations are way off for what should be blending and what shouldn't be. Let's first set the center of the joint as shown in Figure 7-43.

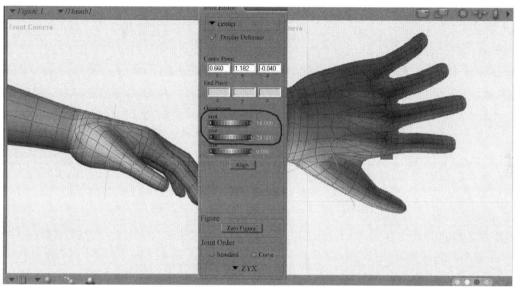
Fig 7-43

Note the settings for the xRotate and yRotate in the orientation box. These need to be set manually to approximately 16 for X and 24 for Y because the Align button will not work properly due to the irregular shape of the first joint of the thumb. If you look at the zRotate (Twist) of the first joint now, you will see it moves better but it still grabs way to much of the side of the hand all the way down into the index finger. So let's adjust the include and exclude for the zRotate and see if that helps.

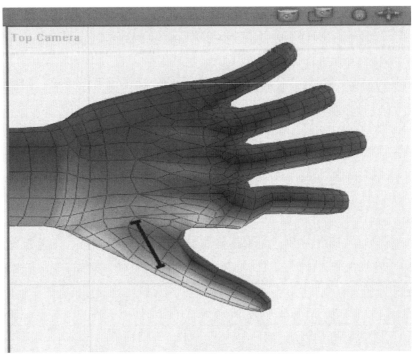

Fig 7-44

 A setting as shown in Figure 7-44 helps but the Index finger is still distorting so we will have to use the SFZs to isolate the joint further. Go ahead and click the box for the Spherical Falloff Zones on the zRotate in the Joint Editor.

We'll need to set the Front Camera view to Main Camera and center it so that we have a good full body view as shown in Figure 7-45. You'll see that the SFZs are grouped together at the feet of the character. Select the outerMatSphere from the Props menu and use the Properties trans dials to move it to the same location as shown in the right hand image of Figure 7-45.

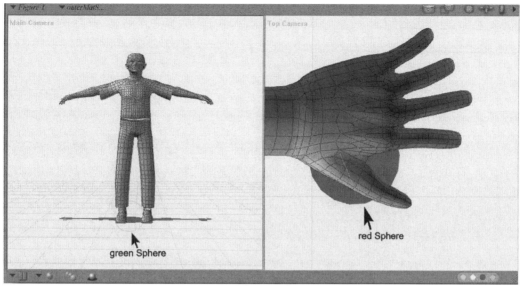

Fig 7-45

You will note that when you move the sphere on the X and Z Axis that it moves according to the orientation of the joint: at slight angles. Also you need to rescale the sphere to about 4 percent on the xyz Scale dials. Once you get the sphere up around the first thumb joint you can switch the Main Camera back to the Front Camera for fine tuning the location of the outerMatSphere as shown in Figure 7-46.

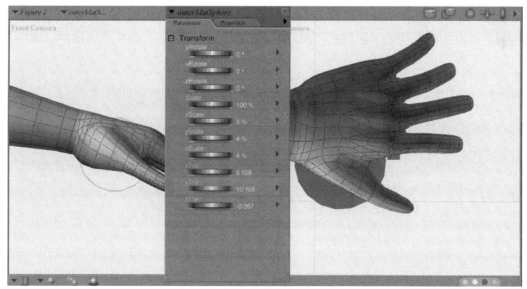

Fig 7-46

We can now select the innerMatSphere from the Props menu and use the same settings as those for the outer to get the sphere quickly positioned for fine tuning as shown in Figure 7-47.

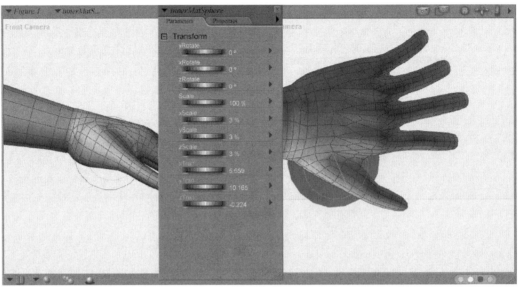
Fig 7-47

As you can see when it is in position the innerMatSphere should be about 1 percent smaller than the outer and moved out along the joint a little farther to allow the blend zone between red and green spheres to work. Now try the zRotate for lThumb1. I think you'll find it works

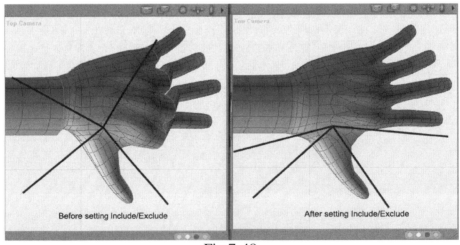
Fig 7-48

much better now.

The yRotate setting for lThumb1 is just a minor adjustment of the include/exclude angles as shown in Figure 7-48.

The xRotate for the lThumb1 will need to have the SFZs set but you can use the settings for the zRotate as a starting point to speed up the process. The final joint setting will look something like Figure 7-49. Note that I switched the Front Camera view for the Left Hand Camera for setting the include/exclude angles.

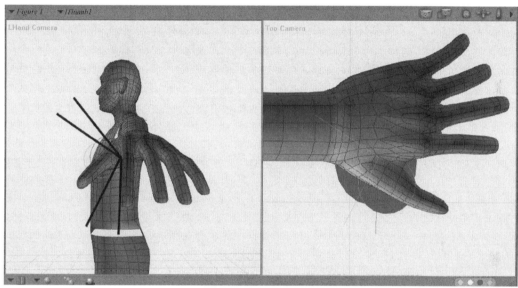

Fig 7-49

For the 2$^{nd}$ and 3$^{rd}$ joints of the thumb, move the cross so that it is centered in the joint, hit the Align button on the Joint Editor, check the rotations, and move on. It's pretty much that simple.

Now let's look at the first joint of the Index finger and use it as an example of the first joint of all the fingers.

First let's look at the xRotate. OK, we looked at it let's move on. What? Why? If you can find ANYONE who can twirl their fingers around on what would be the xRotate (Twist) axis, I'd really like to meet them.

The yRotate is pretty much just a setting of the exclude angle to stop the hand and other fingers from being drug along with the side to side motion. A good setting is similar to the one shown in Figure 7-50.

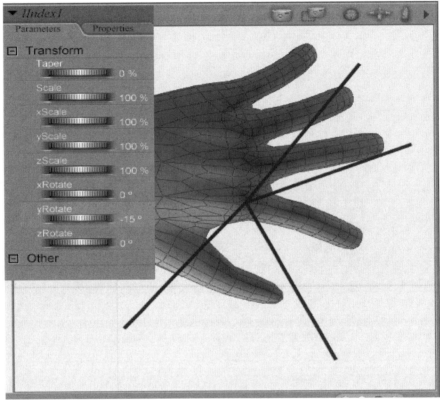

Fig 7-50

As you can see this was set with the finger positioned at -15 degrees on the yRotate so adjust accordingly if you set it when the joint is 'straight'.

The only rotation that really matters for the fingers is the zRotate or the Bend. Although we have some movement from side to side (spreading the fingers apart) most of the movement is bending into the palm to grasp objects. If you bend (zRotate) the lIndex1 joint you will see it affects almost all of the fingers across the hand even after setting the orientation alignment for the joint. So we will have to make adjustments with the SFZs to isolate the joint as shown in Figure 7-51.

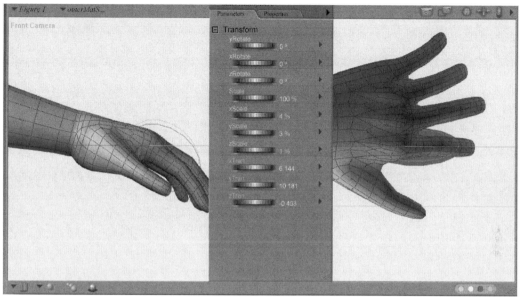
Fig 7-51

To get these settings very quickly I just copied the settings from the first joint of the thumb for the inner and outer spheres and then made adjustments on the trans location and sizes until I found a combination that allowed the joint to move freely on the zRotate without affecting the other fingers. This same process can be used on the other first joints but be aware that you'll need to make slight orientation adjustments on the yRotate axis to align the joint since each of the other fingers bend slightly to the rear. These alignments would be as shown in Figure 7-52.

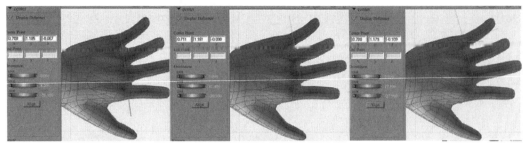

Fig 7-52

For the remaining joints of the fingers, select them one at a time, get the cross centered on the joint fairly well, hit the Align button on the Joint Editor and move on to the next one. This will give you a pretty good starting point that you can refine in terms of the orientation of the joint if you want to.

Before we move onto the next section you are probably wondering why I am so loose in setting many of my joint parameters. This is because many of the parameters don't have to be set to the nth degree of perfection simply because if you use the joint limits, many of the problems associated with 'extreme' positions vanishes because your character can't reach those positions ... and most probably a real person can't reach them either. Although setting limits is an optional process I have provided a chart that lists a good starting point for the joints of this character. These can also be used as a reference for other characters that are similar in body design. In this chart I also list the proper name that is associated with the joint rotation so that you can change that too while changing the minimum and maximum limits of the joint rotation. To change these settings, select a body part and double click on the rotation dial you wish to edit. A dialog panel like the one in Figure 7-53 will be displayed.

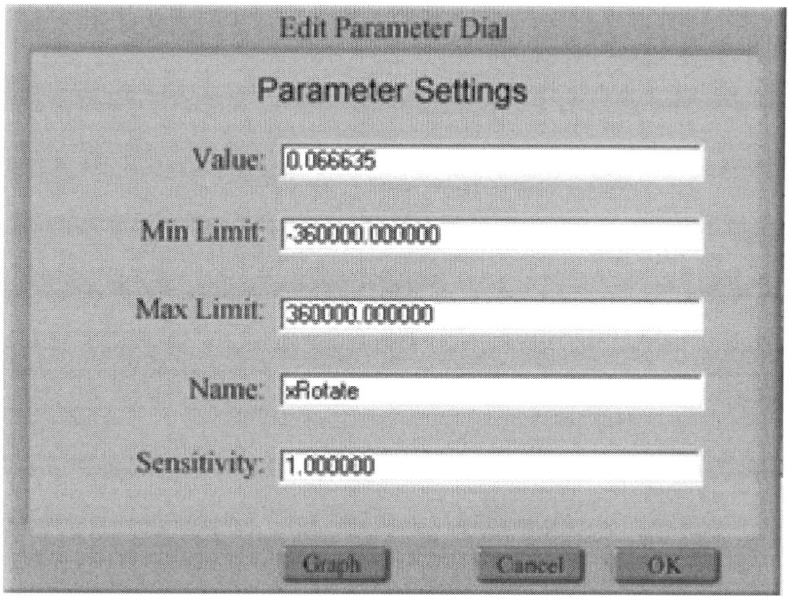

Fig 7-53

Enter the Min Limit and Max Limit in the box provided and then rename the Dial to the name you want to use or the one shown in the chart provided. After these are set, click OK to save the changes.

Do this for each joint and each of the xyz rotations of the joint on both sides of the body.

We are now done setting joints.

What? We didn't set the joints for the right hand side? Well, we could start from the beginning of the chapter and work our way down the right side or ... we could just select Figure from the drop down menu, click Symmetry and then click Left to Right. When you are asked if you want to copy the joint setup zones, click yes. Now you are done with the right hand side of the body. Note: While this copies ALL the joint settings, it does not copy and name changes you made to the dial names. You still need to rename them one by one down both sides of the body.

Before saving HomelessJoe to the runtime, be sure to memorize all the settings we have made using the Edit > Memorize > Figure command from the menu options.

# Chapter 8: UVs
# To Map or not to Map

It's not really a question. If you want your characters to have more than one color, you're going to have to do some type of texture map to allow for it. Basic UV mapping is not that hard and you can do a pretty good job of it with the Classic Version of UVMapper. We'll be mapping Homeless Joe, so let's go ahead and get UVMapper fired up and load the OBJ for Joe.

When last we left our intrepid adventurer in UVMapper, he looked something like Figure 8-1.

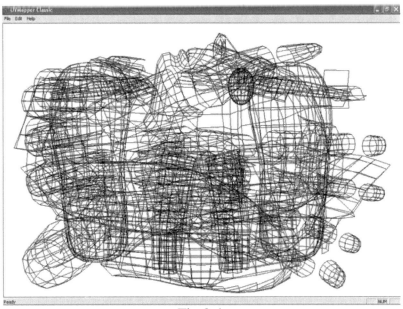
Fig 8-1

Not a very functional map for painting textures on. But we have to start somewhere. Some of you may ask why we didn't do this while breaking Joe up in the first place. And the answer is we could have. But I like to wait until I have a character in Poser and rigged before I start working on UVs only because during the rigging process you may make a change or two to the mesh that will affect the UVs and you end up having to do more work on them to fix what was changed. It's just easier to wait until the figure is pretty much set in stone in Poser before meshing with the UVs.

Let's start by having a good look at Joe front and back. In the Edit menu select New UV Map > Planar and just click OK. Z-Axis is fine and we want to split the map front to back now.

The display should look something like Figure 8-2. In fact, you could even use this AS your map. But you'd find it hard to paint and have any kind of real details.

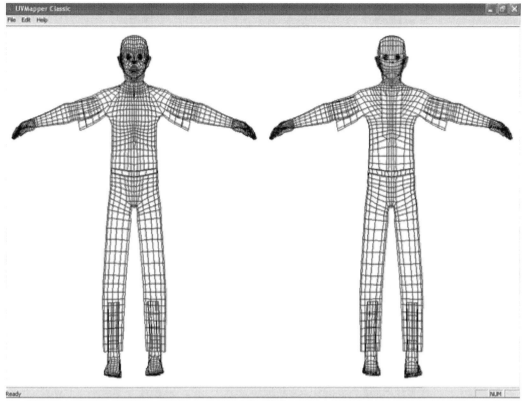

Fig 8-2

Looking at the character from this point of view, we can quickly see what some of the material zones we will need are. First we have to separate all the skin areas which will include the head, neck, portions of both arms and both hands. Also, we will want to establish a material zone for the shirt, one for the pants, shoes, and probably the 'socks'. Additionally we will want to separate the eyes from the head and name material zones for the whites and the iris for each eye. So we are looking at about 7 material zones named: skin, shirt, pants, shoes, socks, eyes, iris. So let's start by grabbing the easy stuff first and creating a few material zones to start off with.

In the Edit menu, select Select > by Group. You will get a dialog box with a scroll bar listing all the body parts. For our first material zone, let's name what we can for the skin. In the slider menu listing click on the head and then hold down the Control key so we can select additional body parts. Scan down through the list and select anything that can associated with the skin material. This would include: head, neck, both forearms, and the hands and fingers. We don't want to include the shoulders yet because they are combined material zones of both the skin and shirt. After all of the easy 'skin' parts are selected, click OK and they will be highlighted in red as indicated by the bounding box in Figure 8-3.

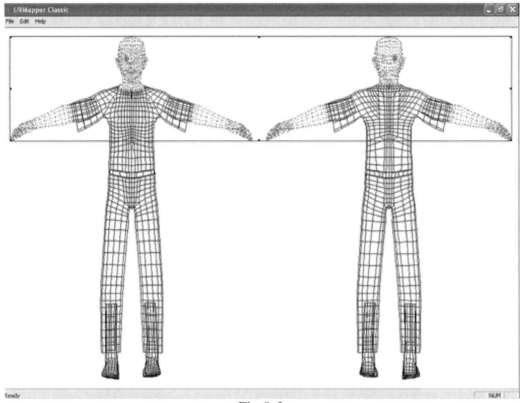

Fig 8-3

With these selected, use the Edit > Assign > to Material command to assign them to a material named skin. After naming the material, click Ctrl+{ to make those parts invisible.

Now let's name the first group of the shirt material. Again, select Edit > Select > by Group and from the list select the chest, abdomen, and the right and left collars as shown in Figure 8-4.

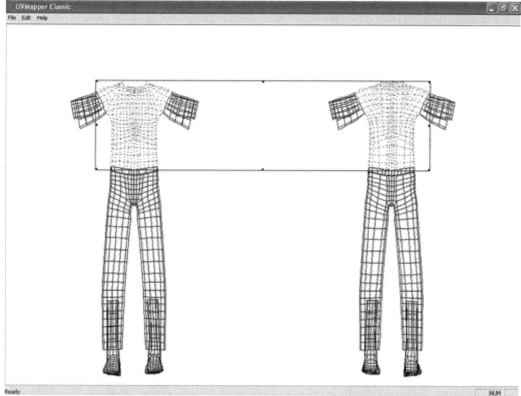
Fig 8-4

Using the Edit > Assign > to Material command, name these parts to the shirt material and then click Ctrl+{ to make them invisible.

Now let's name the first grouping for the pants. In the Edit > Select > by Group, select the hip, and left and right thigh as shown in Figure 8-5. And then assign them to the material name of pants.

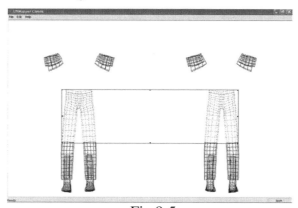
Fig 8-5

While still selected, click Ctrl+{ to make them invisible.

Now select the feet and toes as shown in Figure 8-6.

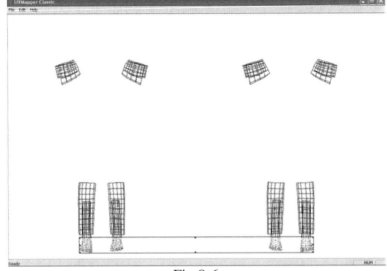

Fig 8-6

And assign them to the material shoes and make them invisible.

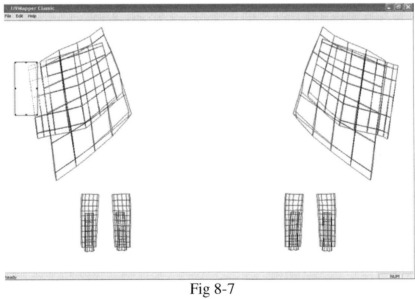

Fig 8-7

At this point all we have left on the screen are the shins and the right and left shoulders. Let's do the shoulders first. Drag a selection box over them and using the Edit > New UV Map > Planar command, leave the alignment on the Z-Axis but now select Don't Split. Resize the resulting image so that it fills the upper most part of the screen as shown in Figure 8-7.

As shown before, carefully select the parts that would be assigned to the skin material and move them to a clear space on the screen. Do this for both collars so that you have a collection of polygons similar to those shown in Figure 8-8.

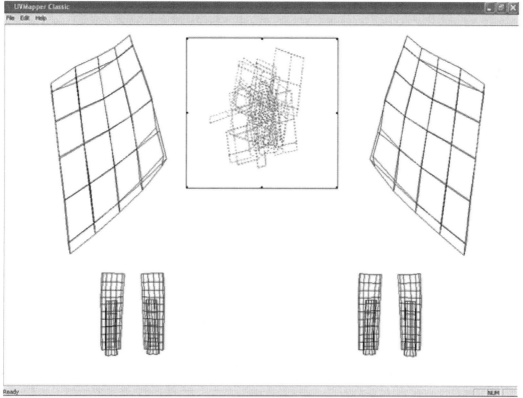

Fig 8-8

As shown, select and name the group to the skin material and make it invisible. Then select the remaining portions of the collars that are part of the shirt and name them to the shirt material and make them invisible.

As with the collars, now select the shins and use the Edit > New UV Map > Planar command to set them as an Don't Split view on the Z Axis. With the new map, grab the resize handles and size the display of the shins so that it fits most of the display as shown in Figure 8-9.

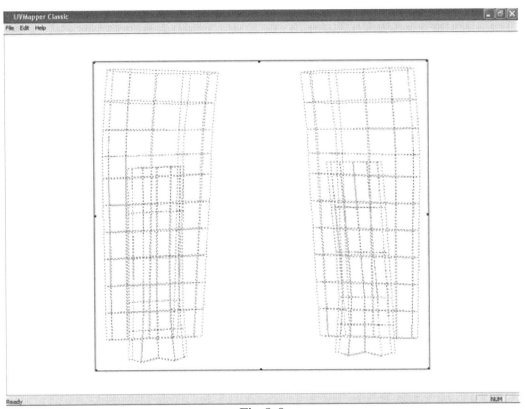

Fig 8-9

As with the collars, carefully select out the parts that need to be assigned to the socks material and place them in an open space as shown in Figure 8-10.

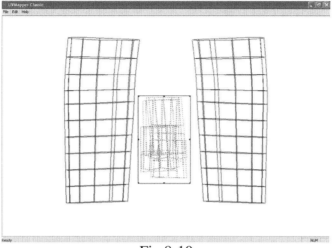

Fig 8-10

Select the socks and assign them to the material socks and then make them invisible. Finally select what is left of the shins and assign them to the pants material. Make this invisible too.

All that is left to do now is name the parts of the eyes. I save that for last so that you could get a little experience selecting easy parts and separating them for naming to materials.

From the menu select Edit > Select > by Group and then select the head. A selection box will appear on the screen where the head is located. Click Ctrl+} to make the head visible. Now resize the selection box so that it covers a good portion of the screen and then from the menu click Edit > New UV Map > Planar and make sure the X-Axis is selected for Alignment and that Don't Split is selected. You should have an image similar to Figure 8-11 now.

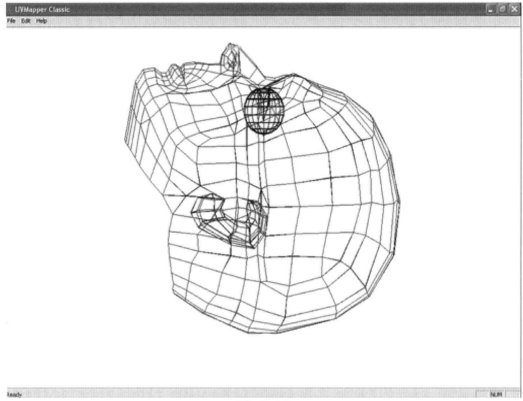

Fig 8-11

From this view you can easily see the heavy lines of the eyes and we should be able to pull out most of the parts. But let's do it backwards. Let's remove everything that isn't part of the eyes and move it off to

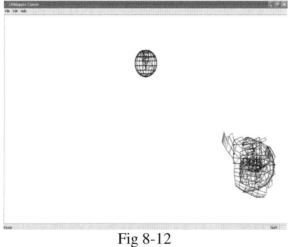

Fig 8-12

one side. So carefully select parts of the head around the eyes and move them away and shrink them down so that they aren't in the way as shown in Figure 8-12.

Now select the eyes and resize them so they fill most of the clear area of the screen. From this we should be able to pull out the remainder of what isn't eye and now we have a clear view as in Figure 8-13.

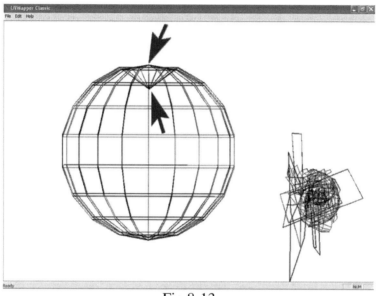

Fig 8-13

Note where the arrows are pointing? These represent the tips of the two cones that make up the iris of both eyes. Carefully select each of these and slide them off to a clear area of the screen as shown in Figure 8-14.

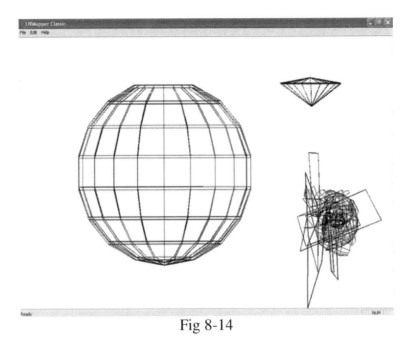

Fig 8-14

Now select the portion that represents the white part of the eye and assign it to material eyes. Then select the portion that represents the iris of both eyes and assign that to the material iris.

With no polygons selected, click Ctrl+{ to make everything invisible.

Now select each material one at a time from the Edit > Select > by Material command and make that item visible. Assign a final UV Map to it, usually Z aligned and Split by Orientation, and then size it and place it where you want it on the screen for later painting the texture. Do this for each material making sure they don't overlap. My arrangement is pictured in Figure 8-15.

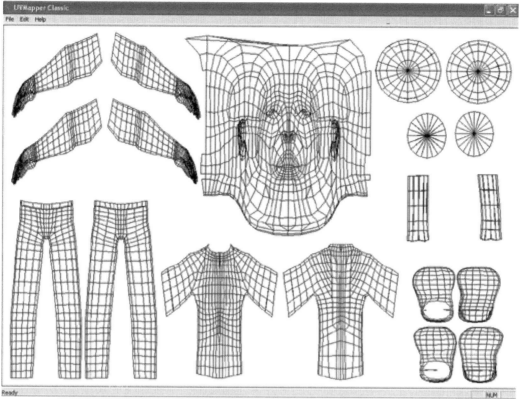

Fig 8-15

This map covers all the basics pretty nicely. All of the parts are oriented on the Z Axis and split front to back except for the face and feet. The feet are oriented on the Y Axis and split top and bottom while the face is unwrapped using a spherical map on the Y Axis. Also, note that the eyes and the iris' are NOT split. Some people like to separate the hands and position them for painting with more details. This model doesn't really require that as all skin is going to be painted a single color so there won't be issues with the map stretching and distorting.

Once you are happy with the layout, save the model back to the Obj to insure the UVs are saved with the model and then save a copy of the map to the BMP format in the same folder.

## Chapter 9: The Color of Joe

Painting textures for Poser characters is something that an entire book could be written about. For some it's like a religious experience or on par with the creation of a final CG image. Let's face it, a bad texture can break a great character and a good one can save a bad character. A lot of people use high power programs like Photoshop or PaintShopPro. In fact, I use Photoshop for most of my work. But these programs cost money and in the vein of 'beginners doing this for free' idea that I approached the book with, I wanted to find a good paint program that was free and I felt comfortable recommending to people for painting textures. I knew of a lot of shareware programs, but I wanted something that was truly free ... open source. And I found it.

**Artweaver:**
For anyone who has used Photoshop, this program will look familiar. It is an excellent Photoshop clone with just about as much power and

performance but with no price tag attached to it. Below, Figure 9-1, is a picture of how it looks on my dual screen system.

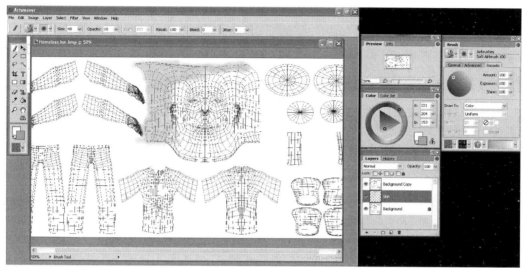

Fig 9-1

Of course my screen is actually in color but you get the idea. Figure 9-1 was actually made in Artweaver. Pretty much everything you need to produce professional level texture maps for Poser characters can be found in this program.

Let's take a look at the basics you'll need and how to use them in an efficient way.

Layers – Artweaver supports standard type layering just like Photoshop and PSP. When you first bring a UVMap image into Artweaver you'll want to make a copy of the background image by right clicking Background in the floating Layers menu shown in Figure 9-2.

Fig 9-2

Right click the Background Copy and from the menu select Properties and set the transparency of the layer to around 50%. This will give you a nice ghost map over all the work you do. But remember to see the work in FULL color you have to turn the Background Copy layer off by clicking the EYE icon next to it in the menu.

Now, using the menu option shown in Figure 9-3, create layers for each of the materials and name them for that material.

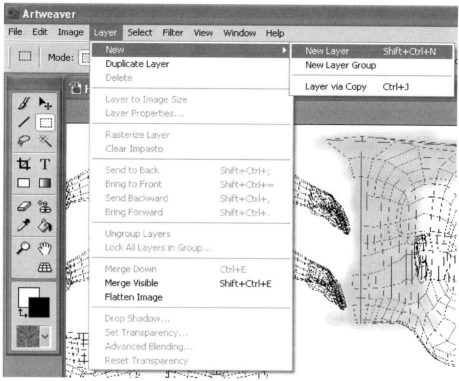

Fig 9-3

Everything else is pretty much play and discover what you can do with this program. You could use it to paint very basic color maps for Joe or explore the textures and various brushes that are supported via the floating Brush menu. You can also try different paper textures to see how that affects the look of your texture. The choices are so many and so varied that it would take another book to explore them all. So I will leave it to you to explore, or use your own favorite paint program to make the textures for Joe.

# Chapter 10: Conclusion

Well, all that remains is to put it all together. By that I mean apply the textures you create to Homeless Joe and start posing him and rendering pictures with him. And then get going on your very own project.

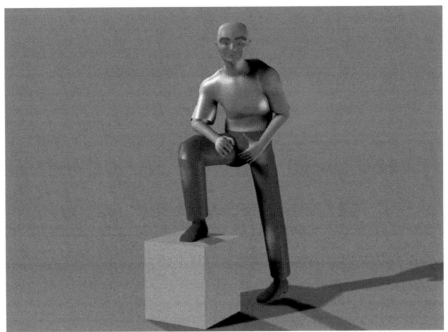

My final version of Joe looks like this.

Some issues you may run into while working through the projects in this book are as follows:

1. Scale – Poser uses a scale that can be radically different from other programs. It is not unusual to bring a character into Poser using the PHI file system and having the character way too large to even fit on the screen. There are several ways to fix this. Obviously, you can use the character scale on the Body and shrink the character down. But this can create issues when you try to set the joints. You

can also bring the mesh into Poser first and save back out right over the top of the original before doing any work on the mesh. This will sometimes correct the scale of the mesh. Another way is to bring the model in through the PHI file, scale it down to the correct size, and save the OBJ back out over itself again and then bring the model back in again using the PHI file. This method sometimes leads to the issue described in #2.
2. Doublets – After creating a character and getting it rigged, when you load the OBJ into UV Mapper to create the UV Map, you will notice that sometimes there are doublets of the body parts. For example: abdomen:1 and abdomen:1 abdomen.  This is caused by Poser when saving an OBJ. I think it has something to do with saving an OBJ into itself. It is probably best to save to another name and then delete the original and rename the saved one to the correct name. Another way to fix this is to go into the Poser Grouping Tool and combine the like names together and then deleting the duplicates.
3. Reversed Normals – Reversed normals are probably my greatest pet peeve in Poser. Fixing them can sometimes be a real pain in the Poser. The easiest way is to just click the Normals_Forward box on the materials pallet for a specific material. This only reverses the normals at render time though, so while you are posing the character, the parts will still be inverted. Another way is to use the Grouping Tool and carefully select the offending parts and reverse them. This can be quite a challenge sometimes. The pay version of UV Mapper includes a tool for looking at and correcting the direction of the normals too. As does the shareware tool AccuTrans 3D. Many 3D modeling programs also support this to varying degrees.

Well, that about covers the basics. I hope you didn't find this too complicated and maybe just a little bit fun. I'd love to see what you come up with and feel free to send me pictures at:
<u>dadchamp1@gmail.com</u>

Also feel free to send questions and comments too.

# Addendum: Poser 8 My Character

With the introduction of Poser 7 there was little of anything new under the sun so it was decided that an update to this tutorial book would not be needed. But with the advent of Poser 8, enough has changed that an addendum to the book to include some of the new features of Poser 8 was decided.

At first glance there doesn't appear to be a whole lot different in Poser8 until you move the mouse to a friendly location and what used to be there has been moved. The new interface, Fig P8-1, is

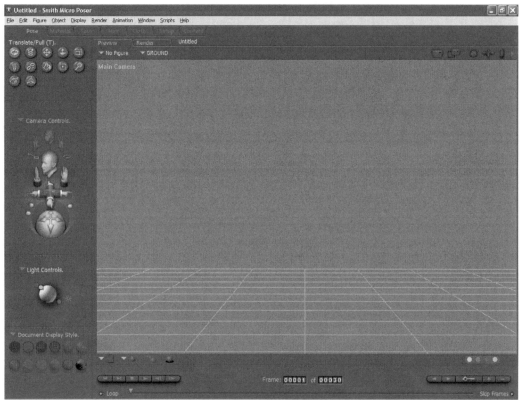

Fig P8-1

completely modular and be torn apart and rearranged to the users desire. All parts of the screen can be docked or floating and this comes in very handy for people with multiple monitors, allowing for a much more clean look and feel than previous versions.

One of the biggest changes from previous versions, and part of the reason for this addendum, is the updates to the Setup Room. See Fig P8-2.

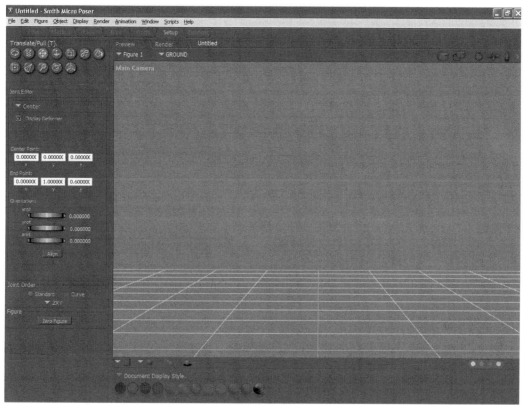

Fig P8-2

Now, in addition to having the boning tool, the Joint Editor has been moved into this window to allow for easy access while using the Setup Room. But since this book avoided the Setup Room in favor of a more traditional, and easily understood method, this is of little use to people who are in the learning the process. Additionally, the Joint Editor in the Setup Room does not interact with joints in the same was as described in this book. While testing a joint for proper blending, joints will not move and display blending properties while in the Setup Room. For this reason I still recommended to do ALL final joint setup and blending outside of the Setup Room.

Besides adding the Joint Editor to the Setup Room several very nice features have been added to the Joint Editor too. All of these have to do with upgrades to the Falloff Zone system. See Fig P8-3

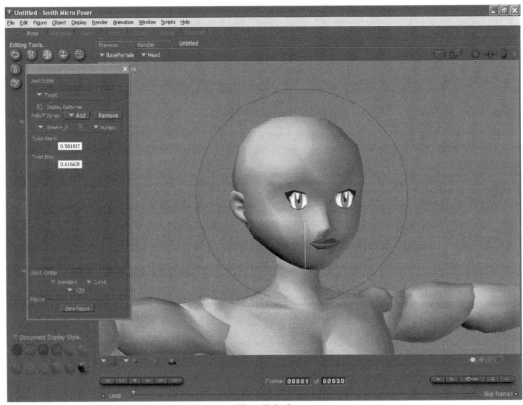

Fig: P8-3

Above you can see what at first seem like minor changes to the Joint Editor pallet when a rotation is selected. In this case the head is selected for the Y or Twist rotation. As in the old system directly below the selection box for the Joint Rotation is the check box to select whether to display deformers or not. But now below that is a new area that adds the ability to Add or Remove Falloff Zones and directly below that is displayed the currently active Falloff Zones. See Fig P8-4 for a more detailed view.

As you can see in this detailed view the Falloff Zones button for Add activates a drop down menu for the different Falloff Zones that can be added to a joint. These now include the classic Sphere and the new Capsule Zones as shown below in Fig P8-5. Of special note is that now when you add a Falloff Zone it is partially centered around the joint area it will be affecting. This a major boon from previous versions where the zone was dropped to the ground between the feet and had to be manually moved to the proper location of the joint.

Also, with Poser 8, you are now able to apply multiple Falloff Zones to each joint rotation so that difficult joints for blending can be improved by expanding the areas blended with multiple Falloff Zones.

Fig: P8-4

Fig P8-5

Additionally each Falloff Zone applied to a joint can be set to Add or Multiply the effect of the Zone. I have been experimenting with this process and as of yet have not really noticed any eye popping effects. But the option of additional Falloff Zones per joint rotation offers interesting possibilities when refining a joints blending abilities.

Of course as, with most options within Poser 8, the ability to Cancel the process of adding a Falloff Zone to a joint is offered in the drop down Menu too.

After adding a Falloff Zone to a joint rotation you can now, also, decide whether the effect of the Blending will be an Add effect or a Multiply effect as shown in Fig P8-6.

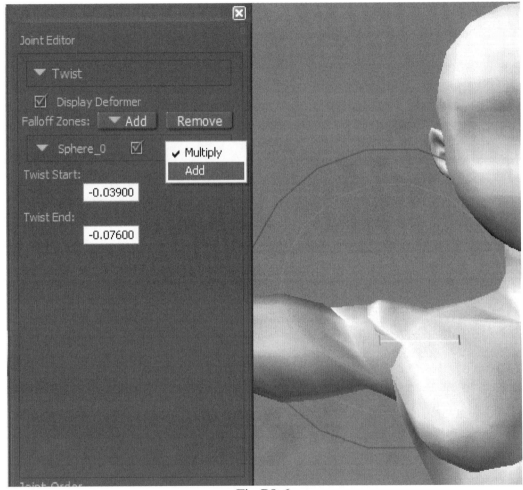

Fig P8-6

The Multiply Effect is standard to Poser and is what has been used in all versions that have allowed the setting of Falloff Zones. This setting has a cumulative effect on all areas between the red and green spheres and allows for fine blending on most joint areas. The new Add Effect is much more direct and noticeable in how it affects a joints Blending. Where Multiply would give a gradual merging of two mesh areas at a joint, Add would give hard, well defined areas that in many instances would be far to harsh for a standard Falloff Zone. I have discovered the Add effect works well with extra zones in addition to the standard ones defined in this book and gives the user some very nice tools for creating muscle bulges in and around joint areas that are many times considered 'difficult' joints. IE: The collar/shoulder areas and the hip/thigh areas.

The new Falloff Zone, the Capsule Zone, is a much needed and long requested addition to the setup tools for a Poser character.

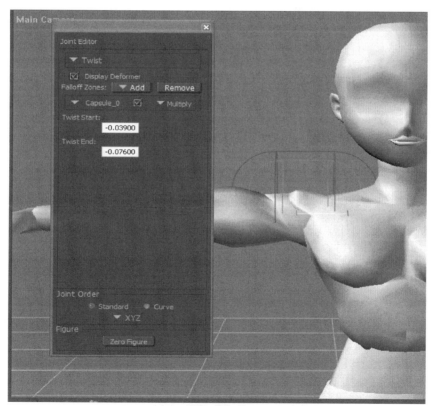

Fig P8-7

As shown in Fig P8-7, this Falloff Zone is a cylinder that is rounded at both ends making it ideal for long blending areas that require a gradual effect not achievable with the standard sphere. It also allows for some very exotic blend zones in that both ends can be sized and shaped independently. Thus allowing for the restriction and fine addition of blend areas not available before as shown in Fig P8-8 below.

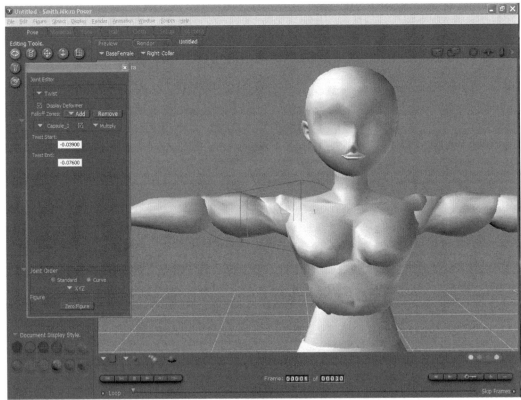

Fig P8-8

In this instance the shape of the capsule has been redefined into a cone that follows the shape of the arm more accurately and allows for a much more accurate blending in the zones along the Twist or X Axis of the Collar. Capsules can also have one end reversed creating an hourglass shape with a negative space in the center. This is useful when blending is wanted at both ends but not in the middle of a joint. Capsule Zones are also very nice for doing joint refinements with the Add function to create areas of defined muscle bulging in a joint.

As you can see in Fig P8-9, in addition to the regular sizing and positioning dials for the blending zones, there are also dials related to resizing the ends of the capsule to create cones and key hole shapes that allow for much more refined blending zones.

I know I haven't nearly covered as much new information as I should or would have liked to have done in this short addendum, but with Poser8 still being fairly new, I am still learning many new things about the additions to the tools for creating characters. As with any book like this, it is a work in progress and as I become more comfortable with my knowledge and use of the new tools provided in Poser8 (and more and better

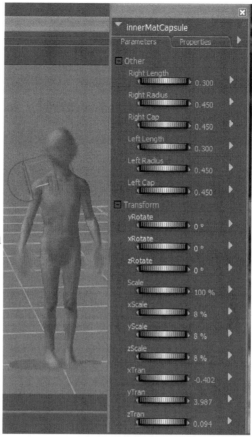

Fig P8-9

understanding of the older tools and tricks I discover along the way) I will continue to update this volume with that information for the people who want to create their own Poser content.

## Joint Limits Reference Chart

| Body Part | Rotation | Name | Min | Max |
|---|---|---|---|---|
| Head | yRotate | Twist | -35 | 35 |
| | zRotate | Side-Side | -8 | 8 |
| | xRotate | Bend | -35 | 20 |
| Neck | yRotate | Twist | -35 | 35 |
| | zRotate | Side-Side | -35 | 35 |
| | xRotate | Bend | -40 | 25 |
| Chest | yRotate | Twist | -25 | 25 |
| | zRotate | Side-Side | -20 | 20 |
| | xRotate | Bend | -20 | 45 |
| Abdomen | yRotate | Twist | -25 | 25 |
| | zRotate | Side-Side | -15 | 15 |
| | xRotate | Bend | -20 | 55 |
| lThigh | yRotate | Twist | -30 | 30 |
| | zRotate | Side-Side | -10 | 20 |
| | xRotate | Bend | -95 | 65 |
| lShin | yRotate | Twist | -25 | 25 |
| | zRotate | Side-Side | -5 | 5 |
| | xRotate | Bend | -15 | 120 |
| lFoot | yRotate | Twist | -15 | 15 |
| | zRotate | Side-Side | -8 | 8 |
| | xRotate | Bend | -25 | 40 |
| lToe | zRotate | Twist | -5 | 5 |
| | yRotate | Side-Side | -10 | 10 |
| | xRotate | Bend | -30 | 20 |
| lCollar | xRotate | Twist | -20 | 20 |
| | yRotate | Front-Back | -40 | 20 |
| | zRotate | Up-Down | -35 | 65 |

| Body Part | Rotation | Name | Min | Max |
|---|---|---|---|---|
| lShldr | xRotate | Twist | -45 | 40 |
|  | yRotate | Front-Back | -60 | 20 |
|  | zRotate | Up-Down | -35 | 20 |
| lForeArm | xRotate | Twist | -20 | 20 |
|  | zRotate | Side-Side | 0 | 0 |
|  | yRotate | Bend | -150 | 15 |
| lHand | xRotate | Twist | -35 | 85 |
|  | yRotate | Side-Side | -15 | 15 |
|  | zRotate | Bend | -35 | 60 |
| lIndex1,2,3, | xRotate | Twist | 0 | 0 |
|  | yRotate | Side-Side | -8 | 8 |
|  | zRotate | Bend | -75 | 5 |
| lMid1,2,3 | xRotate | Twist | 0 | 0 |
|  | yRotate | Side-Side | -8 | 8 |
|  | zRotate | Bend | -75 | 5 |
| lRing1,2,3 | xRotate | Twist | 0 | 0 |
|  | yRotate | Side-Side | -8 | 8 |
|  | zRotate | Bend | -75 | 5 |
| lPinky1,2,3 | xRotate | Twist | 0 | 0 |
|  | yRotate | Side-Side | -8 | 8 |
|  | zRotate | Bend | -75 | 5 |
| lThumb1 | zRotate | Twist | -30 | 20 |
|  | yRotate | Side-Side | -30 | 20 |
|  | xRotate | Bend | -15 | 40 |
| lThumb2,3 | xRotate | Twist | 0 | 0 |
|  | yRotate | Bend | -5 | 55 |
|  | zRotate | Side-Side | -8 | 8 |
|  |  |  |  |  |

# Acknowledgments

A special thanks goes out to Steve Cox for letting me include a copy of UVMapper Classic with the resources for this book. Be sure to visit his website:

www.uvmapper.com

And be sure to download the demo of UVMapperPro and check it out. It is a program well worth the money if you find the Classic version not powerful enough for your needs.

Also a big thanks to Roy Riggs for writing the PHI-Builder program way back in 1998. It's still a trooper today. Visit his website:

www.royriggs.com

And drop him a note to say thanks. (A Special note to Mac users: To my knowledge there is nothing like PHI-Builder for the Mac. Although Poser in the Mac does allow for building characters using a PHI file, the file has to be written using a standard text editor and saved with the '.PHI' suffix.

And finally, a thanks to Boris Eyrich for his work on Artweaver. Stop by his website:

www.artweaver.de

And bookmark it for future updates to this wonderful, FREE, paint program.

# Copyrights

Poser – eFrontier/Smith Micros
Photoshop – Adobe Systems Inc.
PaintShopPro – Corel
Maya/3DMax – Autodesk Inc.
Lightwave – NewTek, Inc.

Any other software mentioned is copyrighted by their respective owners

# Resources

All the resources used in the projects in this book are available as a FREE download from Content Paradise:

http://www.contentparadise.com/productDetails.aspx?id=10490

This file includes the OBJs for BoxMan, TinyDancer, and HomelessJoe. It also contains copies of UVMapperClassic, PHI-Builder, Artweaver and some FREE animation samples from Eclipse Studio (www.es3d.com).

Printed in Great Britain
by Amazon.co.uk, Ltd.,
Marston Gate.